GOD GIVE US CHRISTIAN HOMES

HOPKINS
publishing inc.

P.O. Box 3687
Cleburne, TX 76033
HopkinsPublishing.com

Copyright © 2015 Jim Faughn
ISBN-10: 1-62080-049-7
ISBN-13: 978-1-62080-049-2
Library of Congress Control Number: 2014947061
Version 1.0

eBook:
ISBN-10: 1-62080-050-0
ISBN-13: 978-1-62080-050-8

Discover Other Titles
By Hopkins Publishing
HopkinsPublishing.com

DEDICATION

This book is dedicated to the cute girl who first caught my eye when I was a junior in high school and she was a sophomore, Donna Carol (Turner) Faughn. Half a century later, she still catches my eye.

The reasons are too numerous to mention, but, suffice it to say that a Christian home would not have been possible without her. What a blessing she is to my life, the lives of our two children, our son-in-law, our daughter-in-law, and our five grandchildren.

It is no exaggeration to say that she blesses every life she touches.

Table of Contents

An expert is one who has done something well enough to know what he/she is talking about - in Jim Faughn we have living proof that what he says rings with truth. First of all because he has saturated it with the Word of God (which is enough for most of his readers) but in addition to that every member of the Faughn family is a testament to the effectiveness of these teachings.

The principles are simple but not simplistic and the book is written in an engaging style. Jim demonstrates that an extreme careful reading of the text reveals much insight. The fruit of his study reveals much that I have never considered and wish I had known years before. "Christian Homes" is interspersed with humor and illustration ample enough to keep any reader engaged.

Every church library should have a copy of this book. Read it yourself and you will find yourself thinking about buying a copy for young couples just entering marriage or becoming first time parents. It would be as good a gift as you could give them."

–Dale Jenkins - The Jenkins Institute

INTRODUCTION

As we worship, we often sing *God Give Us Christian Homes*. That thought is both the title of this book and the desire of its author.

This book may not be adding anything profound to the countless sermons, books, articles, lectures, etc. that have preceded it. It may serve only to remind us of some very important things that appear to have been overlooked and/or ignored by many in the world, our own society, and (regretfully) many who wear the name "Christian."

While many words have been written and spoken about families, there are still a variety of reasons for the writing of this book. Among those reasons is the fact that, seemingly all that has been written and/or spoken has not helped to heal many of the ills found in far too many families.

Christian homes do not just happen merely because we may sing about them or because we merely express a desire for them to exist. There are things that should, and must, be done in order for them to exist.

It is my prayer that *something* in this book will help *somebody* in their relationship with the members of their families. In addition to that, it is my prayer that these words will help the reader to develop and nurtures a close and personal relationship with "...the Father of our Lord Jesus Christ, from whom the whole family in heaven and earth is named" (Eph. 3:14-15).

Jim Faughn

The Bible's First Love Story

The Bible's First Love Story

I have noticed one interesting fact about most of the material I've read about the home. There seems to be the absence of a good love story.

Years ago, Tina Turner recorded "What's Love Got to do With It?" One might get the idea from reading some of the material about the home, that the answer would be, "Nothing at all."

That seems to be the case especially as we let the world define the word "love." Love is usually portrayed as being all about emotions, romance, physical attraction, etc. Sadly, there seems to be little, if any, material in books and other things written from a Christian perspective about these matters.

Every generation seems to believe that it is the first to discover romance. Every generation also seems to believe that it has the right to define that term. To members of one generation, romance could be all about a man going out of his way to protect the woman. To another, romance could be about candles, soft music, etc. Yet another generation could define romance as something that only involves a physical attraction.

About all that each generation has in common with other generations is that it believes it has found some new insight on this idea that their parents and others have somehow missed. After all, what they see from their parents doesn't look very romantic to them.

Consider the dilemma of the young person who grows up in a home where he/she sees the following from the parents: they always seem to be talking about serious things; they go through the same daily "grind" of employment, housework, paying bills, etc.. Then, as the sun goes down, they fall asleep in front of the television. It is not difficult to imagine the confusion in the mind of this young person.

The confusion could get worse when this young person goes into Bible class or hears some preachers. It is easy to get the idea that the subjects of dating and marriage are all about rules, restrictions, and emotionless relationships. That certainly doesn't sound very romantic.

This young person knows what is expected of a Christian in the dating relationship. He/she knows that people who love him or her expect purity. It is also stressed that God expects purity.

This young person also knows that God and others have certain expectations when one enters into the marriage relationship. Foremost among these is that each partner is to remain "faithful" to the other for a lifetime. It is repeatedly stressed that any deviation from that standard is severely frowned upon; to say the least.

When our hypothetical (but very typical) young person thinks about how the word and concept of marriage is often used by those who teach from the Bible, it does, indeed, sound very emotionless and not very appealing. He/she remembers hearing the mention of some man giving his daughter in marriage to another man. *That* certainly doesn't sound very romantic.

It seems that the physical relationship is glossed over in terms of a man "knowing" his wife. What does that mean? Is there any romance in this? One might even get the idea that the only reason for this relationship is so that children can be born which, in turn brings about more "rules and regulations."

While our young person is struggling with these concepts and with his or her own sexuality and identity, there is abundant information coming from other sources. Unless he or she lives in a cave somewhere and has absolutely no contact with the outside world other than "going to church," he/she is bombarded with the world's view of love, sex, romance, marriage, etc.

This view is all about the physical and emotional.

In this view ---

> ...when the lovin' starts,
> and the lights go down,
> there's not another living soul around,
> then you woo me until the sun comes up,
> and you say that you love me.

These words, recorded by Fleetwood Mac a number of years ago in their song, "Say You Love Me," sure sound more romantic and exciting than two people going to sleep in front of a television.

At the same time, there are some very strong implications that the view of love proposed in this song is, like much of what is presented by the various media of our day, quite a bit different than God's view of love. I don't think that anybody would argue that God's view of *any* kind of love would cause somebody to include these words from the same song: "...if you use me again it'll be the end of me."

I can think of no scenario wherein God would suggest that one person should be "using" another person. This would apply to every relationship; especially the family relationship.

While it may surprise some people, God's view of the love that can exist between a husband and a wife does not preclude some of what the world would view as romance. There actually is some material in God's word that puts these two concepts together. While we do not want to take up the space here to explore each instance of that, we will, in this chapter take a look at what I believe is the Bible's first love story.

The material is found in the book of Genesis. It involves two people; Jacob and Rachel. While most of the material we will be looking at is found in the twenty-ninth chapter of Genesis, we will also be making some reference to chapters twenty-eight and thirty, as well as other passages from God's word. People other than Jacob and Rachel also play a role in this fascinating account.

Chapter twenty-nine of Genesis begins in what looks to be a fairly straightforward manner. It almost looks like we are reading a Sergeant Joe Friday "just the facts ma'm" verse when we read, "So Jacob went on his journey and came to the land of the people of the east" (Gen. 29:1, all references to scripture are from the New King James Version unless otherwise noted).

In the margin of one of the Bibles I use, there is a "further explanation" of the word "went" in that verse. According to the note, in the Hebrew language this could be rendered, "lift up his feet." It has been suggested by some that the meaning of this could be that Jacob was "kicking up his heels" or "stirring up some dust."

Why all of the excitement? Why would he make such a long trip and not have any complaints? Why would a man make such a trip *even if he did have some complaints?*

There appear to be two answers to those questions. The first is to be found in the latter part of chapter twenty-eight. He was assured that God would be with him on his journey. God promised him the land he was in and told him:

Behold, I am with you and will keep you wherever you go, and will bring you back to this land; for I will not leave you until I have done what I have spoken to you (Genesis 28:15)

The second reason is found earlier in chapter twenty-eight. *Jacob was on his way to find a wife!*

This fact may raise another question. Why was it necessary to travel so far in order to find a wife? Were there not any "eligible" women where Jacob was?

To find the answer to that question we need to read the last verse of chapter twenty-seven:

And Rebekah said to Isaac, 'I am weary of my life because of the daughters of Heth; if Jacob takes a wife of the daughters of Heth, like these who are the daughters of the land, what good will my life be to me' (Genesis 27:46)?

We know from earlier material in Genesis that Rebekah was not without fault. One of her mistakes, of course, was that she openly demonstrated favoritism between Jacob and Esau. One would almost have to be paying no attention to the biblical record to miss her obvious preference of Jacob over his brother, Esau.

Rebekah's consternation over the daughters of Heth could be seen in this light. It could be seen as no more than the thought that "none of these women around here are good enough for my favorite son."

However, if for no other reason than just the sake of another consideration, let me suggest another possibility. I believe that it is entirely possible (and I prefer to believe that this is a better explanation) that Rebekah was concerned that her son would marry somebody with similar values as those she tried to instill in her son. Of utmost importance would have been the fact that a husband and wife would begin their life together worshiping the same God.

In a later chapter, we plan to discuss the father's role in the home, but we get some insight into it here. I find it interesting that Isaac did not call for Jacob and say something like, "Your mother and I have been discussing this and **she** has some criteria in mind about the kind of woman you should marry." Neither did he say something along the lines of, "Jacob, your mother and I have complete confidence in your judgment. Whomever you choose to marry will be fine with us."

As chapter twenty-eight of Genesis opens, Isaac, **the father**, is taking the lead in setting some guidelines for who his son will marry. There are some really practical lessons in this.

Even though this account is thousands of years old, some modern fathers could learn a lesson from this. Our responsibility goes much further than just "putting food on the table." This will be explored a little further later on, but, for now, we need to plant the seed that Dads should play a major role in child-rearing and the guidance of those in their families.

Dads and Moms can, and should, work together in ways similar to the way in which Isaac and Rebekah worked in this instance. Their partnership was not without its challenges and was, at times, far from being perfect, but, in this instance it can serve as a model for twenty-first century parents.

We will also be discussing the role of children in the family later, but one factor is evident here. Jacob was certainly old enough to believe that he had the right to make up his own mind about things that pertained to his life. I'm sure he could play the "I'm old enough to make my own decisions card" more effectively than most who try to use that one today.

However, Jacob respected and went along with the wishes of his parents. The parent-child relationship is a two-way street. The parents, of course, need to do their best to fulfill their God-given roles. At the same time, the children need to see what God would have them to do in this regard and to demonstrate the proper respect for their parents.

This series of events in Jacob's life contains some more information which I believe to be of a practical nature even today. He knew where he was going to find a wife and had a general idea of what type of woman he would find. When he got to where he was going, he found a woman there who looked attractive to him.

Somebody might wonder at this point where I get the idea that Rachel was attractive to Jacob. I readily admit that I'm "reading between the lines" here, but I don't think I'm reading too much into the text.

It seems evident that things really got moving "...when Jacob saw Rachel..." (Gen. 29:10). He had been told about her (v. 6) and had found out that she was a member of the right family (vs. 5-6), but it seems to me that he really sprang into gear when he actually saw her for himself.

Why did he volunteer to remove the stone from the well? Could it not have been an attempt to get rid of the shepherds so he and Rachel could be alone?

What's all the running and kissing about in verses 11-13 if there was not some type of emotion involved? Did Jacob weep after he kissed Rachel because she was not very good at that kind of thing, or because he had found exactly what he was looking for?

It is not just the figment of some romance novelist's imagination that, sometimes, there is such a physical attraction between two people when they first meet that "bells go off." There *is* such a thing as "love at first sight."

Those who may read these words and who have not, at this point in their lives, found a marriage partner could learn a lesson from Jacob. They need to consider where they are going to be when "that certain someone" walks into their lives. Will they be in the wrong place, with the wrong atmosphere, and the wrong kind of people when that happens or will they be in a Christian environment with people who share their same values and commitment to God? The only sure way to know is to keep company with the right kind of people!

There is absolutely nothing wrong with having and maintaining standards about the one with whom you will share your life. Loneliness is often not pleasant, but living an entire lifetime with the wrong person could very well be much worse.

If, as we have suggested, there was something special about the first time that Jacob saw Rachel, we might wonder what role, if any, physical attraction plays in a relationship. We would be beyond naïve if we were to believe and suggest that physical appearance and attraction plays no role in the dating and/or marriage relationship.

However, all one has to do is to look at old pictures to see how the aging process affects our physical appearance. When the wavy hair has waved good-bye, the twinkle in the eye is from the line in the bifocals, and you are suffering from "Dunlap Disease" (that malady where the belly has "dun lapped" over your belt), is there still room for romance and/or any of the other factors that make for a good marriage?

What about somebody not blessed (cursed) with tremendous physical beauty to start with? Is there any hope for us?

I may be reading more into the description of Rachel and her sister, Leah, than I need to, but there may be some suggestion here as to why Laban had such a difficult time "marrying off' his older daughter. There is no doubt about the physical qualities of Rachel. Every translation I have checked agrees with the New King James Translation that "...Rachel was beautiful of form and appearance" (Gen. 19:17).

However, the translators are unsure about the description given to Leah in that same verse. Below are some of their efforts to translate the first part of Genesis 29:17:

Leah was tender eyed... (KJV)

Leah's eyes were delicate... (NKJV)

And Leah's eyes were tender... (ASV)

Leah's eyes were weak... (RSV, ESV)

And Leah's eyes were weak... (NIV)

There is also an interesting factor with regard to the meaning of the names Rachel and Leah. Rachel means, or is taken from the word, "ewe." One wonders if she saw that as a compliment or not.

One does not have to wonder about Leah, though. There are several suggestions as to the derivation of her name and none of them would be a compliment to anybody. According to various sources, the name "Leah" can mean "weary," "dull," or "wild cow." None of those choices would be very desirable to a young lady.

If, in fact, there was a discrepancy between the physical appearances of these two sisters and if Leah did not have the physical beauty that Rachel had, this might be a good place to remind ourselves that "...the Lord does not see as man sees; for man looks at the outward appearance, but the Lord looks on the heart" (1 Sam. 16:7).

This verse, of course is part of the selection process during which David is chosen to be the second king of God's people. It might also be helpful to remind ourselves of the tribe from which David came. It might also be helpful to remind ourselves from which tribe the priests were to come. It is of great interest, at least to me, that Judah, from which tribe David and subsequent kings were chosen and Levi, from which tribe the priests were chosen were both the sons of Leah!

If Leah was not a striking physical presence as seems to have been the case with Rachel, that did not keep her and her descendents from playing a major role in the history of God's people. All too often today, people are chosen to be a mate **and** to fulfill various roles in the church based primarily on physical qualities. What a shame!

The continuing story of Jacob and Rachel demonstrates to us that romance and commitment are not mutually exclusive. They can, in fact, co-exist in the same relationship.

In some materials in my files, Dr. David Thomas reports on a study by Dr. Elaine Walster. Dr. Walster interviewed or observed more than 100,000 people.

> She found that, for most couples, intense passion lasts six months to two and a half years. Clearly, for love to persist, it has to move beyond that first romantic frenzy into a warm intensity of deep friendship.

We have made much of the fact that "...Jacob saw Rachel..." (Gen. 29:10). That same verse also informs us that he saw "...the sheep of Laban his mother's brother."

It could be that the entire account of Jacob's attraction to, and relationship with, Rachel was an attempt to "get into the will." Maybe, she was his ticket to increasing his material assets and that was all she meant to him.

In fact, there seems to be some interest in the material things on the part of Jacob. After all, he sure worked a long time to "get what was due him" in the way of material things.

If the only reason that Jacob was interested in Rachel was to have access to some material possessions, their final separation from her father would have been a good time to finally end that relationship, but he did not do that. In fact, there is evidence that suggests that the "love story" between these two continued throughout her lifetime – and beyond.

Genesis 35:16-20 records the death and burial of Rachel. The fact that there was still a physical attraction to her on the part of Jacob is suggested by the fact that she died giving birth to Benjamin. The account of her burial, though brief, indicates that Jacob wanted to pay tribute to the woman he loved deeply. Even years later, as Jacob is preparing to bless the sons of Joseph, he makes sure that Rachel receives mention in the story of his life (cf. Gen. 48:7). She was not forgotten, but was lovingly remembered.

We have the opportunity to see "true love stories" like the one recorded in the opening book of the Bible in our own communities and in our present day. Some of these stories are being lived out in your neighborhood; some in a nursing home or an assisted living facility in your community; some may be in your own family.

When you find one of these "true love stories," you are likely to find two people stooped by that aging process. One of them may be pushing the other in a wheelchair;. There is nothing really attractive about either of them. In spite of all of this, the love they have for one another is very obvious.

Like the account of Jacob and Rachel, their story is true *and* it is about true love. Although nobody else may understand what they see in each other now, they are setting the example for us every day.

Decades ago, one or both of them "caught the eye" of the other. At first, that may have been the only attraction, but they began to talk and spend time together. As they did this, they found out they really had a lot in common. Along the way, he asked her *the question.* She said "yes" and they've been Mr. and Mrs. ever since.

Years ago, "their song" was probably upbeat, romantic, and looked to the future through rose-colored lenses. Now, the song written by Albert Rosell could be "their song." It sure beats many of the tunes that pass for love songs in terms of painting a picture of real love.

SHOULD YOU GO FIRST
Should you go first and I remain
To walk the road alone,
I'll live in memory's garden, dear,
With happy days we've known.

In Spring I'll watch for roses red
When fades the lilac blue,
In early Fall when brown leaves call
I'll catch a glimpse of you.
Should you go first and I remain
For battles to be fought,

Each thing you've touched along the way
Will be a hallowed spot.

I'll hear your voice, I'll see your smile,
Though blindly I may grope,
The memory of your helping hand
Will buoy me on with hope.

Should you go first and I remain
To finish with the scroll
No length'ning shadows shall creep in
To make this life seem droll.

We've known so much of happiness,
We've had our cup of joy
And memory is one gift of God
That death cannot destroy.

Should you go first and I remain
One thing I'd have you do;
Walk slowly down that long, lone path,
For soon I'll follow you.

I want to know each step you take
That I may walk the same.
For someday, down that lonely road,
You'll hear me call your name.

If
I Choose
To Marry

2

If I Choose To Marry

An elder where I once preached had what some people might consider a typical family. He had more children (five) than the average family today, but, other than that, his family was fairly normal – that is until one began to examine his family just a little "below the surface."

Along with his five children, he had three step-children. His wife had lost her first husband earlier in life and had, sometime later, met and married the brother who was now serving as an elder in the Lord's church.

The part of his story that some apparently found unusual was not the number of children in the family. Nor was it even that he had children and step-children. That is an increasingly more common situation in our society.

What surprised some people was that our brother *waited until he was thirty-nine years of age to get married.* He used to tell me that, as he entered his late twenties, early thirties, and even mid-thirties, people would ask him why he had never married. He told me once, "I never thought about the fact that I hadn't married. I just thought that I hadn't married **yet**."

Is there a "right age" for two people to enter into a marriage relationship? Is there a "typical" marriage? Is marriage something God expects of us or is it a choice? Does God have the right to regulate this arrangement and, if so, what are some of those regulations?

It might be appropriate, at this juncture, to mention some of the criteria which will not be used here. Four such criteria come to mind very easily.

First, **grandma** will not be used to determine the truth about this important subject. Grandmothers have a way of "explaining away" all sorts of activity (or inactivity) on the part of their grandchildren. Grandma's house may be a pleasant place to go for cookies and hugs, but it may not be the best place to go for an unbiased opinion on some subjects.

Secondly, we will not be discussing or using as a yardstick **what exists in some family or families**. I believe that all of us have had the experience of knowing members of families who have drastically changed their thinking on a variety of subjects merely because a child, a sibling, or another member of the family had pursued a particular lifestyle. Most of us have probably even seen family members try to defend, or at least overlook, a living arrangement that is clearly contrary to God's will just because somebody close to them has begun living that way.

Society condones a lot of things that it used to frown upon. Because of the "shifting sands" of what society considers as moral, this cannot be used as an adequate standard. It appears to me that we may have difficulty using this "standard" at all. The standards set by society seem to change more often than does the direction of the wind and they seem to be constantly blowing in the wrong direction.

Finally, we will not be using as a criterion **what is legal**. One can keep both the letter and the intent of the civil law and still violate God's law. Allow me to suggest a couple of examples of this.

First, the most liberal interpretation of what God has to say in His Word about the consumption of alcoholic beverages will allow for the fact that *drunkenness* is a sin. While it may be argued (incorrectly in my view) by some that drinking in moderation is not condemned in the Bible, it is commonly agreed that one has "crossed the line" if he or she has drunk alcohol to excess.

Now, suppose that I were to tell you that, in the privacy of my own home and with nobody else around, I had the habit of becoming so intoxicated that I could no longer properly function. What law have I violated? There could be no charge of "public indecency or intoxication." I could not be charged with DWI or DUI. Although I had broken no law, would you not agree that I had sinned?

What about the Nuremberg trials of Nazi officials following World War II? Were they tried because they had violated German law? No; they were following German law. Neither were they tried and convicted because they had violated the laws of the United States, Great Britain, or some other nation. These people were tried and convicted because of the recognition of a "higher law."

It is that "higher law" which shall be the criterion used in this chapter. It is my firm conviction that God *does* have the right to regulate marriage and has done so in His Word. While this chapter cannot (and is not designed to) answer every question or to deal with every situation which may present itself, we will try to consider some of the things found in the Bible about marriage.

We believe that the answers to some of our questions are in, or are at least hinted at, in the very first text in God's word that suggests a husband-wife relationship:

> And the Lord God said, "It is not good that man should be alone; I will make him a helper comparable to him."...And the Lord God caused a deep sleep to fall on Adam, and he slept; and He took one of his ribs, and closed up the flesh in its place. Then the rib which the Lord God had taken from man He made into a woman, and He brought her to the man...Therefore a man shall leave his father and mother and be joined to his wife, and they shall become one flesh (Gen. 2:18-24).

"Therefore" is, of course, the first word in verse 24. The often expressed "rule" about the word "therefore" is to find out *what it is there for*. It appears to this observer that this word, and its placement, hints at the fact that marriage can be considered an option and not a requirement.

The verses immediately preceding verse twenty-four have to do with man's need for companionship. Many have found this need to be met in the marriage relationship.

However, it is my observation (and I believe that it is the teaching of scripture) that marriage is not a requirement for companionship and/or fulfillment.

Please do not misunderstand. I am, in no way, talking about or defending co-habitation or any other arrangement that is clearly outside the will of God. What I *am* saying is that some people can and do find fulfillment in life without a spouse.

Have we forgotten some of the material Paul was inspired to write in 1 Cor. 7 & 9? We will not take the space to investigate these chapters in any detail, but we hope that the reader will read them and see that Paul, in no way, considered marriage as a requirement for one to serve or to please God. In fact, he makes it very clear in these chapters that he had the right to marry, but had not taken advantage of that right in order to devote his life in service to his Lord in a way that was most fitting for him. We believe that the reader will find our Lord addressing this in a somewhat different (but similar) way in a conversation He had with his disciples in Matthew 19:10-12).

If, then, I make the choice to marry, is there any information I can glean from the Genesis account of the first man and first woman on the earth? More pointedly, is there any information in Genesis 2 that would help my marriage and all marriages even today?

I believe that the answer to both of these questions is an unqualified **"Yes."** It seems to me that there is a great deal of information in these few verses. This information is not only helpful, but vitally needed today.

First, it is obvious from this reading that marriage is designed by God for a male and a female. There was a time when this was a "given" in our society and in most societies. Sadly, this is no longer the case.

Most of us are only too well aware of the impact that the "gay lobby" has had on our politics, our society, and even among some who would bristle if you refused to refer to them as Christians. As I type these words, "marriage" between two people of the same sex is legal in thirty-seven of our fifty states. Even though we may be becoming increasingly marginalized, it is our duty to remind people that homosexuality has been, is, and always will be condemned by the One who created a woman as Adam's wife (cf. Gen. 2:22-24).

What about the "right" age for marriage? Was that elder I mentioned earlier too old at thirty-nine? Did one of my uncles "wait too long" when he married at age fifty-three? What about a couple I once knew who were fifteen and fourteen when they married? Is that too young? Apparently, they did not think so. They had two sons and served the Lord together for more than half a century (until the death of the wife).

When our children were growing up, I used to kid them that I might think about letting them start to date when they were in their thirties. While their mother and I did not stick with that, we did set what we thought was a more realistic age of sixteen.

Were we too lenient? Were we too strict? Again, what is the appropriate age for dating and marriage?

Various societies, families, and even religions have grappled with those questions for centuries. Those questions will not be answered in this space, but we believe that there is a clue about a general guideline in Genesis 2.

It will be noticed that Adam and Eve were not created as children, but as a man and a woman. It will be remembered that, when they were created, they had the ability to reproduce (cf. Gen. 1:28).

It seems to me that God is trying to tell us that marriage is not for children, but for people with some measure of maturity. While the record provides for us no magic age, it does give us a clue or two about the appropriate level of maturity.

I believe the record suggests (and multiplied experiences demonstrate) that people who enter into the marriage relationship need to be mature enough to "…leave…father and mother…" (Gen. 2:24). A friend of mine and a brother in Christ is from a family of seventeen children. He told me once (and I *think* he was joking) that, when one of the siblings left the home to get married, somebody cut off the part of the table where he/she had sat so they couldn't come back to eat!

While I do not believe that God wants the separation from parents to be this drastic, to say the least, I do believe that the husbands primary earthly responsibility is to his wife and the wife's is to her husband. The word God used is "leave," not "abandon."

While this will be discussed in a later chapter, we need to say at this point that parents, especially older parents, are *not* to be abandoned by their children. We remember Joseph's concern for his father and the rest of his family as well as the fact that Peter's mother-in-law was sick and was *in Peter's house*. (cf. Gen. 42-47; Luke 4:38-39).

Sometimes the maturity level of an individual can be seen is his/her temperament. If he's a spoiled brat and/or if she is still daddy's little girl, the marriage will experience some very rocky days. If he thinks its "manly" to explode in a fit of rage at every inconvenience and/or if she pouts at every imagined instance of inconsideration, maybe they need to mature somewhat before they try to make a home.

The word "cleave" is a vital part of the passage under consideration and a vital part of making any marriage "work." The word used here has to do with the process of bonding materials together.

The marriage relationship is to be a bond in the best sense of the word. Those who enter this relationship should already have their minds made up that, when time has taken its toll on their appearance, they will stick together and stick it out.

Sometimes the situation is much more serious than just the normal aging process. An accident, a serious and debilitating illness, and/or any number of other things can turn the person one marries into somebody barely recognizable. What then?

Will we be like the man I read about whose wife had a serious automobile accident that left her horribly disfigured? Will we, like him, walk into our spouse's hospital room and announce, "You are not the person I married!"? Will we then, as he did, turn our back and walk out of the room never again to see the one to whom we made those vows about commitment and caring?

What would you have done if you had been Terri Schiavo's husband? If you remember, this case made national headlines and received so much attention that the president of the United States even got involved. Mrs. Schiavo had been in a "persistent vegetative state" for over a decade before her death in 2005.

The debate raged about whether or not to take her off of life support *like her husband wanted to do.* Those who got all caught up in his emotional statements about "this is what Terri would want" must have missed the fact that her husband had been living with another woman for some time and had children by her. Apparently, there wasn't enough "glue" to make this concept of "cleaving" a reality.

What if the problem is not physical changes? What if one or more of the children cause the family a great deal of heartache? What if a child dies? Marriages have ended because of feelings of guilt, one partner blaming the other, and/or any number of other factors during times like these.

It seems to me that a very important factor in all of this is *time.* Most types of glue and other adhesives I know anything about need time to function as they should. The same is true in the marriage relationship. It is not just the passing of time that is important, but time spent together; time spent talking, sharing, experiencing, and growing.

Though this aspect is not discussed in Genesis 2, it seems that the concept of maturity may also extend into the area of finances. How many young couples do you know who are seriously in debt very early in their marriages because they want what their parents and grandparents have worked and saved for years to have? Good, solid marriages are those in which the people involved work on this together (as they do all the other challenges they face).

How much money should we have **before** we marry? Again, there is no hard and fast rule to this, but the following advice that I picked up somewhere needs to at least be considered:

> If he ain't got nothin' and she ain't got nothin'
> Don't wed.
> 'Cause nothin' plus nothin' makes nothin'
> And nothin' don't chew like bread.

Thus far, the material we have written has been written with the assumption that two people contemplating marriage have God's approval to do so. We stated earlier that the same One who provided this arrangement for mankind has the right to regulate it. It is my belief that He has, indeed, exercised this right.

It is of interest to notice that, even in the account in Genesis 2 about the first couple, mention is made of father and mother (Gen. 2:24). The implication from this seems to be that a marriage would meet God's approval if both partners have never previously been married. In other words, they are leaving the home of their parents in order to establish their own home and family.

Admittedly, there was no other option for Adam and Eve. The same may not hold true for us, though. It may be the case that I have left my parents, entered into the marriage relationship with my spouse and now find myself single again. My spouse could have passed from this life; he/she may have left me for somebody else; he/she could have just left because being tired of being with me, to pursue a career, and/or any number of other reasons; it could even be that I left my spouse for some reason. The possibilities are almost endless.

Do those who are single again have the right to remarry? If so, does that mean that *everybody* who finds himself/herself in the situation of being single again has the right to once again enter into the marriage relationship?

An argument that Paul uses in Romans 7 to demonstrate the superiority of the law of Christ over the law of Moses is both interesting and informative on one of the points of our discussion. The word picture that the Holy Spirit paints for us in this text is one in which the old law is dead. This frees us to live under the new law.

What is most interesting is how the argument is framed:

For the woman who has a husband is bound by the law to her husband as long as he lives. But if the husband dies, she is released from the law of her husband. So then if, while her husband lives, she marries another man, she will be called an adulteress; but if her husband dies, she is free from that law, so that she is no adulteress, though she has married another man (Rom. 7:2-3).

Again, the Holy Spirit used Paul's pen to inform us that

> A wife is bound by law as long as her husband lives; but if her husband dies, she is at liberty to be married to whom she wishes, only in the Lord (1 Cor. 7:39).

I have read and listened to a lot of "mental gymnastics" about the phrase "only in the Lord." It would be my prayer that no Christian would even consider marrying somebody who does not share his or her commitment to Christ.

What about those who find themselves single again and whose spouse is still living? Again, while there has been a great deal of "mental gymnastics" about this subject, Matthew 19:9 is still in my Bible and is still easy to understand (if not readily accepted in every case):

> And I say to you, whoever divorces his wife, except for sexual immorality, and marries another, commits adultery; and whoever marries her who is divorced commits adultery.

These words from the lips of our Lord are not popular today. Often truth is not popular. Often it is difficult to understand the rationale behind a specific truth. That does not diminish the fact that it is, however, truth.

We will not take the space here to deal with every "what about..." that can and has been raised with regard to Matthew 19:9. Only one will be dealt with here. For far too long many have overlooked the significance placed on *repentance* in God's Word. The short version of this point is that baptism washes away every sin of which one has repented and that God will forgive His children of every sin of which they have repented. If adultery is a sin (and it is) and if I refuse to repent, there appears to be no promise of forgiveness on the part of God.

While this may be seen by some as a "stretch," I hope that I can demonstrate that Henry Kissinger plays a role in this discussion. Many of us remember Dr. Kissinger as the National Security Advisor to one of our nation's presidents and as Secretary of State during the administrations of two of our presidents. We may remember that he was awarded the Nobel Peace Prize. In fact we may remember when one could hardly open a newspaper without seeing his picture or reading something about him.

One might wonder why this man with all of these credentials never served our nation as our president. Why did he not even consider running for this high office?

The answer is very clear. Our Constitution states clearly that a person must be at least thirty-five years of age and must be a natural born citizen of the United States in order to serve as our president. When Dr. Kissinger achieved national prominence, he was already well beyond thirty-five years of age, but he was born in Furth, Germany to Jewish parents who were German citizens.

A person like Dr. Kissinger can apply for (and become) a *naturalized* citizen of our nation, but cannot ever be considered a *natural born* citizen. Consequently, he or she is prohibited by our Constitution from ever serving *in this capacity*.

Dr. Kissinger's career demonstrates that one can find a way to serve, and to do so effectively, even if he or she is prohibited from serving in one particular way. It is hoped that all people will look for ways to serve the Lord in a similar manner and with a similar outlook on life. Does the fact that a person does not meet the qualifications to serve as an elder or deacon mean that they cannot find fulfillment in some other avenue of service? Does the fact that God did not choose to give me the ability to preach or teach mean that I cannot serve Him in some way? If I cannot marry with His approval, does that mean my life is doomed to be unrewarding, unfulfilling, and unproductive?

I may or may not choose to marry. I may or may not have forfeited my right to make that choice, but I can still remember and hold dear the following from the lips of our Lord and the pen of the apostle Paul:

...I have come that they might have life, and that they might have it more abundantly (John 10:10).

...(G)odliness is profitable for all things, having promise of the life that now is and of that which is to come (1 Tim. 4:8).

The
Perfect
Mate

3

The Perfect Mate

number of years ago, I was privileged to hear brother Dan Winkler speak to a group of young people on the subject, "If God Were to Choose My Companion." I jotted down as many notes as I could and tried to "flesh the notes out" from my memory later.

This chapter is the result of brother Winkler's presentation and my attempt to remember some of the things he said. I trust that my efforts in this chapter will not be viewed as an attempt to plagiarize his material. I was just so impressed that I have borrowed from it heavily for this chapter. I have also added a point or two that came to mind as I restudied the passage he discussed.

I am also trying to expand the focus of what was included in brother Winkler's presentation. I believe that there is some material in the text he chose that can, indeed, be used by young people who are considering who will be their partner for life.

I also believe that this material can be used to help those who may be reading this material to do a little self-examination. In fact, the passage of scripture he chose for his text and, thus, the passage that will serve as the foundation of this chapter was originally written to people who were already married.

So, whether you are reading this chapter from the standpoint of one who is looking for a mate or from the standpoint of one who already is a mate, it is my prayer that the following material will be helpful.

The text for this discussion is the material found in 1 Peter 3:1-7:

> Wives, likewise, be submissive to your own husbands, that even if some do not obey the word, they, without a word, may be won by the conduct of their wives, when they observe your chaste conduct accompanied by fear. Do not let your adornment be merely outward--arranging the hair, wearing gold, or putting on fine apparel-- rather let it be the hidden person of the heart, with the incorruptible beauty of a gentle and quiet spirit, which is very precious in the sight of God. For in this manner, in former times, the holy women who trusted in God also adorned themselves, being submissive to their own husbands, as Sarah obeyed Abraham, calling him lord, whose daughters you are if you do good and are not afraid with any terror.
>
> Husbands, likewise, dwell with them with understanding, giving honor to the wife, as to the weaker vessel, and as being heirs together of the grace of life, that your prayers may not be hindered.

The Perfect Mate will Love His or Her Partner More Than Himself/Herself

There is an important, but possibly overlooked, word in verse one and verse seven of our text. That word is **likewise**. This word, like the word "therefore" ties together whatever thought we are getting ready to read with what we have just read.

It seems to me that the placement of the word "likewise" in verse seven indicates that at least some of the material in the preceding six verses can apply to the husbands as well as the wife. We shall explore this in somewhat more detail a little later.

If "likewise" in verse seven ties it together with verses one through six, then the placement of "likewise" in verse one must also tie in the entire discussion with what has been written in the later part of chapter two.

Much of the material we read toward the end of chapter two can be described as an attempt to get the reader to see the importance of what might be called "stepping away from self." That is, we are not to put ourselves first, nor are we to be constantly concerned about "our" rights. We must put others before ourselves.

We invite the reader to read and consider the entire second chapter of 1 Peter and see if that thought does not permeate the chapter. Notice, especially verse twenty. This verse flies in the face of a culture that bristles at every perceived slight, mistreatment, and/or infringement of rights. As one continues to read this chapter, our Lord is presented as the ultimate example of this concept (cf. vs. 21-25).

This should come as no real shock to a Christian. The New Testament is clear in its teaching that becoming a follower of Jesus involves removing ourselves from the throne of our hearts and putting Christ in His rightful place on that throne.

In other words, to use a phrase some are using today, **it's not about me**! The way this translates to our experience as brothers and sisters in the Lord is seen in a variety of places in the New Testament. For example, Paul informs us in Romans 15:1-3:

> We then who are strong ought to bear with the scruples of the weak, and **not to please ourselves. Let each of us please his neighbor for his good, leading to edification**. For even Christ did not please Himself; but as it is written, 'The reproaches of those who reproached You fell on Me' (emphasis added).

It will also be remembered that one of the attributes of love, as described in 1 Corinthians 13, is that is "...does not seek its own" (v. 5). In our relationship as brothers and sisters in the Lord, then, we are to put others ahead of ourselves.

Surely, all would agree that this would also be true with regard to the marriage relationship. As some have observed "we" comes before

"I" in **we**dding. The perfect mate will consider the other person in the relationship before he or she considers self.

The Perfect Mate Will Help his or her Partner go to Heaven

In 1 Peter 3:1, the Holy Spirit uses an interesting word to describe the effect that the conduct of a godly woman can have on her husband. It is said there that her husband "...may be **won** by the conduct of their wives" (emphasis added).

What does that mean? Does it mean that she can win him over to her side? Does it mean that she can win an argument? Or, does it mean something far more important?

Those questions are answered for us in 1 Cor. 9:19-22. In this text, it will be seen that Paul is concerned about "winning" some people or "gaining" them. The word used in this text is the same as the one used in 1 Peter 3:1. If we are in doubt about what he has in mind we have only to read the last verse of the selected passage in order to determine his meaning.

> For though I am free from all men, I have made myself a servant to all, that I might win the more; and to the Jews I became as a Jew, that I might win Jews; to those who are under the law, as under the law, that I might win those who are under the law; to those who are without law, as without law (not being without law toward God, but under law toward Christ), that I might win those who are without law; to the weak I became as weak, that I might win the weak. I have become all things to all men, that I might by all means **save** some (emphasis added).

If, as Paul writes in 1 Cor. 15:33, "...evil company corrupts good habits," what would the opposite of that be? Would it not be true that being around the right kind of people would help me in my relationship with God? Would I not be wise to select a mate and to **be** a mate who helps the other person in the marriage relationship grow closer to God?

All of us recognize that, if one person is standing on a raised podium, and another person is standing at ground level, it would be much easier for the person on the ground to pull the person on the podium *down* to his level than for the person on the podium to pull the other *up* to his level. Why not start a marriage relationship with *both people on the same level* as it relates to their relationship with God?

It is of more than passing interest that even Paul, as he was defending his right to marry (even though he did not exercise that right), described the "proper candidate" as "...a believing wife..." (NKJV) "...a sister, a wife... (KJV). It has been observed by some that, if a person marries a child of the devil, there will always be trouble with the father-in-law!

The Perfect Mate will have The Proper Values

The text we are considering, as well as a number of other texts in God's word, makes it very clear that God is not concerned about what we might call "the externals." What we look like "on the outside" is not nearly as important to Him as what we really are "on the inside."

A couple of very familiar scriptures will suffice to illustrate this principle. The first concerns Samuel's attempt to find and anoint a man to succeed Saul as king of Israel. He thought he had found his man when he saw Eliab. Apparently, there was something about Eliab that must have looked "regal."

However, we all surely remember what God told Samuel about this situation:

But the LORD said to Samuel, 'Do not look at his appearance or at his physical stature, because I have refused him. For the LORD does not see as man sees; for man looks at the outward appearance, but the LORD looks at the heart' (1 Sam. 16:7).

Jesus was also looking at the heart of the some of the Jewish leaders of His day. Repeatedly in Matthew 23 He condemned them for appearing to be one thing while, in reality, being something totally different.

If "the externals" do not matter to God, how important should they be in the marriage relationship? It is clear from the verses we are looking at in 1 Peter that God is more concerned about "...the hidden man of the heart..." (1 Peter 3:4) than He is about those things that are outward adornment (cf. 1 Peter 3:3).

With regard to Peter's inspired instruction to women, he even specifies what qualities are important. It is said that a Christian woman should be characterized by "...the incorruptible beauty of a gentle and quiet spirit, which is very precious in the sight of God" (1 Peter 3:4). The King James translation has the word "meek" for the word "gentle."

While this material is, admittedly, primarily addressed to women, we believe that there are some things contained therein which deserve the attention of men as well. The Greek word which is translated as "gentle" or "meek" in one of its forms in other passages of scripture clearly apply to men and women alike.

For example, Jesus did not say in Matt. 5:5, "Blessed are the meek *women*..." Nor do those things listed in Gal. 5:22-23 as the "fruit of the Spirit" apply only to women. Gentleness (meekness) is in that passage (v. 22). Paul was not addressing only women in Eph. 4:1-2 either when he wrote that this attribute should be a part of the Christian's character. Other verses could be cited, but the point is clearly made in the New Testament that Christians should be gentle or meek.

This same pattern holds true for the concept of quietness. After all, aren't all Christians taught to pray for those in positions of authority in government in order for us to "...lead a quiet and peaceable life in all godliness and reverence" (1 Tim. 2:2)?

Would it not be true that these qualities would positively affect the marriage relationship if both partners could be described in this manner? Wouldn't a gentle attitude diffuse many otherwise dangerous circumstances? Wouldn't many problems be solved or never develop if each partner could learn to quietly listen to the other partner?

None of us want to be in the position of the man who supposedly was asked if it bothered him that his wife always had the last word. His response was, "Bother me? I'm just thankful that the last word has finally come!"

The Perfect Mate will be Faithful

The word translated "dwell" in 1 Peter 3:7 is an interesting word. It is used in the Septuagint (LXX) to mean only to live in a particular house or area. When used in this sense, then, to "dwell together" would mean only to share a house or some other place of abode with another person.

Even without any consideration being given to any intimate physical relationship, it seems that some thought should be given to communication and concern for the other person. That is particularly true when it comes to a consideration of the rest of verse seven.

Without going into a lot of detail, suffice it to say that, in order for marriage partners (or potential marriage partners) to dwell "... with understanding..." (v. 7), a great priority will be placed on sharing dreams, goals, ideals, feelings, etc. Far too many relationships are ruined or never reach their full potential because somebody does not see the importance of communication. All too frequently the reason given by a spouse for unfaithfulness is that he or she has found somebody who **understands** them.

The importance of communication in the parent-child relationship will be discussed in a later chapter, but it also needs to be stressed with regard to the husband-wife relationship. We will suggest later that there are times when it is critical for parents to give their children their undivided attention. The same holds true for marriage partners.

There is absolutely nothing wrong with having interests outside the home. Work schedules, hobbies, etc. can play a legitimate and needed role in our lives as long as they are kept in the proper perspective.

At the same time, we normally marry in order to share one another's lives. This cannot be done without effective communication.

Maybe it would be appropriate to look at our dating experience. Consider the following description of some people's idea of a "date." She is inside the house watching TV, surfing the 'net, or listening to some music waiting for him to pick her up. When he picks her up, he has music (to use a term loosely) blasting away in the car. They go to a movie where they watch and listen to the people on the screen. Then it is back to the car with more music blaring. Maybe they meet some friends somewhere and "hang out" with them before finally concluding their "date." Is it any surprise that, after they get married, one or both of them is surprised that they don't really know one another?

If it is true that we need to communicate when we date, I believe, as suggested above, that it is just as true that we need to continually communicate as husband and wife. Effective communication is not "getting my point across." Rather, it involves listening as much as talking. It also involves observation, compassion and many other things.

Numerous books have been written about effective communication. We would all be well-advised to read and make application of a number of them. None of us want to be like the man who answered the complaint that he never told his wife that he loved her with, "I told her I loved her when we got married and, if I ever change my mind, I'll let her know."

"Dwell" as used in the LXX is not limited to just staying in the same location. It is also used to describe the intimate, physical, sexual relationship between a husband and a wife.

The use of this word in 1 Peter 3:7 indicates to me that there is at least an implied message about sexual faithfulness. It would be beyond redundant to try to reproduce here (or even refer to) all of the passages in the Bible that set forth God's design that the sexual relationship is to be confined to a man and a woman and is to be enjoyed only in the context of a marriage relationship. One example of this teaching would be this thought from Hebrews 13:4, "Marriage is honorable among all, and the bed undefiled; but fornicators and adulterers God will judge."

It seems to me that far too much attention is given many times to trying to look and act attractive to people other than one's spouse. This may be the case at the work place, in social settings, or even at church!

If the same amount of attention was given to trying to be attractive to one's spouse, a lot of problems would be solved. Many eyes may begin to wander just because somebody overlooked this principle.

However, please do not understand this to be an excuse for the wandering eye. There is no scenario that would allow for such behavior with God's approval.

Those who have not yet entered into marriage should look closely at this principle. This can, and should, be seen as a great argument for keeping one's self for a prospective husband or wife. Further, it can, and should, be seen as a very good reason to wait for somebody who has done the same.

I have never understood how somebody could think that a potential husband or wife who has been with other people in a sexual way prior to marriage would automatically remain faithful to one person after marriage. I understand that this does, in fact, happen and I understand the concept of forgiveness. At the same time, serious thought should be given to this before one chooses somebody to marry.

The Perfect Mate Spends Time in Prayer

It is interesting to observe that 1 Peter 3:7 *assumes* prayer. The passage does not suggest something that a husband and wife could consider doing. Rather, it is written in such a way as to help us to understand that prayer is a vital part of one's life.

Husbands and wives need to spend time in prayer. The subjects of their prayer life will be endless. They will want and need to pray for each other, for any children they might have, for other family members, for the cause of Christ, for lost individuals, for our nation and society, and on and on.

It is often said that "the family that prays together stays together." I would add one thought to that. I believe that would hold true more often if those who were doing the praying would make sure that their relationship with God is such that they can actually address Him as "Father."

One of the dangers of Bible study is that one can incorporate some principles of God's Word into his or her life without ever really submitting to the Lordship of Christ and obeying the gospel. For far too many people, the Bible is merely a self-help book. It is designed to be much more than that.

It would be my prayer that all people study the Bible first to make sure that their "vertical relationship" is what it should be. That relationship, of course, is the one with God. After making sure of that relationship, it would be wonderful to make sure that all "horizontal relationships" are what they can be. Our relationships with brothers and sisters in the Lord, people in the community, *and our families* will be enhanced by submitting to the authority of Jesus.

Heirs Together of The Grace of Life

Sometimes, when I am asked to perform a wedding ceremony, I will express to the couple a desire of mine. Sometimes this desire is expressed in a prayer sometime during the ceremony. The desire is stated somewhat along this line: "Now that you have joined hands as husband and wife, I pray that those hands will remain joined as you go through this life and on into eternity."

I am trying to communicate at least a couple of things when I say this or something like this. First, I am trying to get them to remain focused on the Lord and His will for their lives. In the words of 1 Peter 3:7, I am using the phrase "…heirs together of the grace of life…" to mean that each partner can help the other partner to inherit everlasting life. This, as we have suggested earlier, is an important component of the marriage relationship.

However, that is not all that I am trying to communicate. I do not believe that it is all that the Holy Spirit is trying to get us to understand in 1 Peter 3:7 either.

I believe that it is at least implied in this wording that our lives here can be blessed as we work together for a strong marriage. Even if that is not the meaning of this verse, millions of people have found this to be true. They have found that incorporating God's principles into their marriages have blessed their lives beyond expression.

I remember watching a television show about Chang and Eng Bunker. These two brothers were what some call "the original Siamese twins." We still use the term "Siamese twins" to refer to conjoined twins because Chang and Eng were well known and were from Siam (modern Thailand).

I watched in fascination as the television account told of their wives and their twenty-two children (ten children were born to Chang and his wife, Adelaide and twelve were born to Eng and his wife, Sarah Ann). It was interesting to hear of the living arrangements that allowed the brothers to alternate nights between the two farm houses that housed their families. According to the information on the show and some material I've read later, they worked together raising tobacco in North Carolina after their retirement from P.T. Barnum's circus. (It was during their time with Barnum that they adopted the last name of Bunker and gave up their original last name.)

However fascinating that information might be, there is other information about these two men that I find even more fascinating and applicable to our discussion about marriage. First, even with the relatively primitive medical techniques of the time, it would have been fairly easy to separate them. It was their choice to remain conjoined.

Second, the two brothers had totally opposite personalities and habits. One was stubborn and forced his will on others; the other was more passive. One of the twins smoked and drank to excess; the other was a teetotaler. On the television program, it was related that a family member reported on at least one occasion when he walked into a room and found Chang and Eng in a "knock down, drag out fight."

Sadly, I believe that the story of these two brothers finds a parallel in too many marriages. The decision is made to stay together, but the staying together is little more than co-existing at best. It could almost resemble a battlefield where temporary cease fires are observed on rare occasions.

Surely God has something better in mind for us as we choose a mate than that! Surely it is not His intention for a piece of jewelry (a marriage ring) to be the only reason people stay together. Surely there is something more than some vows we barely remember or "the children" that keeps a couple together.

Since it is true that we all sin (cf. Rom. 3:23; 1 John 1:8-10, etc.), there is no likelihood of finding a perfect mate. It is my prayer that the emphasis will be on trying to **be**, not find, a person who will seek to live up to God's ideal arrangement. If both partners in every marriage would have that as their goal, there would be many, many more fulfilled lives and peaceful homes.

The Queen of Creation

4

The Queen of Creation

I't may seem strange to some that we are beginning our discussion of individual roles in the family with women. Some might think that we should start at the top and work down. It may come as a surprise to the people who think that way that this, in fact, may be *exactly what we are doing*.

God's activity in the creation may not be exactly as one four year old girl is said to have understood it. She reported to her mother what she learned in Bible school this way: "God created man; then He took the brain from the man and made woman." While the following is a very loose paraphrase of Genesis 2:21-23, it may come pretty close to explaining the meaning of those verses: "God reached inside of man and found everything He needed to make woman and when the man awoke, he knew part of him was missing."

If one will read the Genesis account of creation, he or she will find something interesting about God's own opinion of what He had done. During His creative work, done during days one, two, three, four, and five, God "...saw that it was good" (Gen. 1:4, 10, 12, 18, 21, 25).

However, things change somewhat, and in two different directions during day six. For the first time, we read where God said, "It is not good..." (Gen. 2:18). Both the thing that was not good and the solution are in the rest of that same verse. The entire verse reads, "And the Lord God said, 'It is not good that the man should be alone; I will make him a helper comparable to him.'"

After God had "topped off" His creation with woman, we read these words: "Then God saw everything that He had made, and indeed it was *very good*. So the evening and the morning were the sixth day" (Gen. 1:31, emphasis added).

Sadly, there are those who believe the Bible to be a continual put-down of women. To them, women are depicted in God's Word as second class people at best and as the property of men at worst.

Nothing could be further from the truth. It is other philosophies and religions which relegate women to second class status. In some cultures women are seen only as a means to an end; that end being the producing of offspring. To the hedonist, she is only a plaything. To the romantic, she is the fairy princess or maiden in distress waiting to be rescued by Prince Charming. The feminist presents a picture of a woman as a self-sufficient career woman, needing no "emotional baggage" like family.

I am unaware of any teaching other than the teaching of Christ that would make a husband and a wife "...heirs together of the grace of life..." (1 Peter 3:7). It should also be remembered that men and women stand on level ground at the foot of the cross (cf. Gal. 3:26-29).

To be sure, some have misinterpreted and/or misused the teachings found in God's Word to assign women to the role of almost (if not altogether) abject servitude. In 1963, Helen B. Andelin wrote a book entitled *Fascinating Womanhood*. While her suggestions may not relegate women to the same status of an indentured slave, some of them come pretty close to doing that. Would all of the suggestions listed below find widespread support in today's society? More importantly, are all of them based on biblical teaching?

DO accept him at face value. DON'T try to change him.
DO admire the manly things about him. DON'T show
   indifference, contempt, or ridicule towards his masculine
   abilities, achievements or ideas.

DO recognize his superior strength and ability. DON'T try to excel him in anything which requires masculine ability.

DO be a Domestic Goddess. DON'T let the outside world crowd you for time to do your homemaking tasks well.

DO work for inner happiness and seek to understand its rules. DON'T have a lot of preconceived ideas of what you want out of life.

DO revere your husband and honor his right to rule you and your children. DON'T stand in the way of his decisions, or his law.

Those who assume that the Bible affirms that women can never have a place of prominence in society and can never make a real impact must have forgotten people like Deborah and Esther. Interestingly enough, both of these women were prominent in the history of God's people in the Old Testament. What makes this particularly interesting is that this is the portion of the Bible that is said to really push women down.

In the remainder of this chapter, we hope to look at some of the concepts found in the passage we looked at in the last chapter, 1 Peter 3:1-7. There is some information here that I believe will be helpful in putting the subject under discussion in the proper perspective.

For example, what is the first thing that many think of when they hear or read the words "weaker vessel" with regard to the wife? All too often, we think of that phrase only as it applies to physical strength. It is generally true that women cannot lift as much, run as fast, jump as high, etc. as men. Is that what is meant by "weaker vessel?"

Some even view this phrase as an indicator of a woman's emotional make-up. Women are often seen as "more fragile" emotionally than men. A lady named Gayle Urban once wrote in *Christian Reader* the following:

While browsing in a Christian bookstore one day, I discovered a shelf of 'reduced price' items. Among the gifts was a little figurine of a man and a woman, their heads lovingly tilted toward one another. 'Happy 10th Anniversary' read the inscription. It appeared to be in perfect condition, yet its tag indicated 'damaged.' Examining it more closely, I found another tag underneath and chuckled – 'Wife is coming unglued.'

While some wives may be becoming unglued, it may have little to do with the supposed fact that they are weaker emotionally than men. It may have much more to do with the treatment they receive from others, in particular from their husbands. In fact the case could be made that, in so many areas, women are stronger than men.

Maybe we've overlooked the fact that the Holy Spirit ties "honor" in with the concept of "the weaker vessel." At our house (and in probably most houses) there is quite an assortment of everyday drinking glasses, coffee mugs, etc. While we try not to abuse them, at the same time, we don't take too much care to overly protect them. When carelessness or inattention results in a crack in one of them, it goes straight into the trash without very much thought.

The same would not be true, though, concerning our more formal dining ware. While we might be guilty of unintentionally banging around some of our "everyday stuff," we would take much greater care of the other plates, glasses, coffee cups, etc. The reason is very simple. The formal ware is worth more in terms of money and it also has some sentimental value attached to it. We might even seek to find some way to repair a broken item.

Isn't that interesting? The cups, glasses, plates, etc. that hold more and can take more abuse are not held in the same esteem as the "vessels" that are weaker in every way!

Could that be behind the admonition for the husband to give "... honor to the wife as to the weaker vessel..." (1 Peter 3:7)? Could the Holy Spirit be trying to get us to see that the wife is the one who "completes the set" and brings out the best in her husband?

What about the concept of submission? In 1 Peter 3:1 & 5 this concept is clearly stated. In the words of v. 1, "Wives...be submissive to your own husbands..."

As the good old boy said, "Mister, them's fightin' words." Surely nobody really expects today's modern woman to be submissive to any man. Some might even go so far as to boldly declare, "No man is going to tell me what to do!"

Really?

If a male dentist tells a woman to "open wide," will she refuse to do so? If a male judge tells a woman to do something, will she refuse? If a male pilot tells female passengers to fasten their seat belts, will they assert their rights and refuse to comply?

It seems to me that, in these scenarios and many more like them, the women would accept the authority and responsibility inherent in the men's positions. They are not admitting that they are inferior in any way. They are just submitting in these instances to somebody qualified in a certain field.

"Qualified" may be a very key word in the previous sentence. No man has the right to demand obedience from a wife merely because he wears the "title" of husband. He must qualify himself to be a husband before he gains her respect. He may find that, as he qualifies and matures even more as a husband, there will be fewer and fewer demands anyway.

We mentioned the necessity of maturity and loving the other partner more than self in chapter three of this book. We will not repeat all of that material. We also will not discuss in detail material which is intended for a later chapter.

However, it must be pointed out at this point that, included in another passage which speaks of the wife's role as being one of submission to her husband, we find an interesting, informative, and challenging concept. The Holy Spirit makes it very clear that marriage is a two way street when He inspired Paul to write, "Husbands, love your wives, just as Christ also loved the church and *gave Himself for her*" (Eph. 5:25, emphasis added).

How much difficulty would any husband have in securing the respect of his wife if she knew beyond any doubt that he loved her enough to die for her? I am convinced that most women would readily and eagerly admire, love, and *submit to* such a man; regardless of how he looked, how much money he had, what his status in the community was, or any number of other factors.

The illustration is old and admittedly well-worn, but it serves the purpose of pointing out the difference between a husband with a warped sense of what such things as love, commitment, and submission mean and what the biblical view of those things are. The illustration centers around a list. This specific list contained those things that a certain husband demanded that his wife do on a regular basis. She did them very dutifully, partly because she knew the consequences of failing to live up to her husband's demands. She also thought she was truly fulfilling her role as a wife in submitting to his demands (and his callousness).

As the story progresses, the husband died and after some time, the widow married another man. This man treated her in a totally different way from her first husband. He treated her like a queen, was attentive to her needs, and demonstrated openly his love and appreciation for her. One day, as she was doing some of the chores around the house, something fell out of a drawer.

What fell out of the drawer was *the list*. She had put the list in the back of a drawer after the death of her first husband and had almost forgotten about it.

As she sat down and read the list she had not seen in years, she burst into tears. She realized she was doing exactly the same things for her current husband that she had done for her first husband. She had never before realized that. Her love and admiration for her present husband made what had been so burdensome before become willing and joyous service to a man who truly loved her.

Submission does not equate with inferiority in any way. To expand on just one of the examples above, the male pilot may be transporting a female brain surgeon to a place where she can perform an operation that nobody else in the world can perform. While she's on the plane, though, she recognizes that her life is in the hands of the man in the cockpit and willingly does what he suggests.

If the person at the top of the organizational chart of a huge corporation is smart, he/she will hire people who are "underlings" on the chart to do things that he or she is not qualified to do. If this president or CEO is really smart, there will be appropriate recognition of that fact and there will be an atmosphere at work that reflects pride in the company and appreciation for people on every level of the chart; including the person at the top.

Try telling a sick child that a mother is inferior! Most dads find out that such is not the case!

It is interesting that Sarah is used as an example of the "submissive wife" (cf. 1 Peter 3:6-7). While it is stated here that she called Abraham "lord" (v. 6), a look at one "chapter" in her life might shed some much needed light on this.

Consider the events recorded in Genesis 21. Specifically, consider the **demand** made by Sarah to Abraham. You can read it for yourself in verse 10, "Cast out the bondwoman and her son; for the son of this bondwoman shall not be heir with my son, namely with Isaac."

Let's look at some of the dynamics of that chapter and of that relationship. First, it is easily demonstrated that Sarah was not some sort of mindless robot. She had definite opinions and was not at all hesitant to express this one – even to the husband to whom she was submissive.

While all of this is true, it is also true that she recognized Abraham's authority to take the action. It should also be observed that, at least in this instance, God agreed with Sarah!

Now, before we get the idea that this incident in the lives of Abraham and Sarah serve to give us the model for the proverbial "domineering wife and henpecked husband," we need to remind ourselves of another aspect of the relationship between these two people. The Sarah who demanded that Hagar and Ishmael be sent on their way is the same Sarah who was willing to pack up everything and move to an unfamiliar place merely because her husband said, in effect, "This is what God wants us do" (cf. Acts 7:1-3; Gen.11:28ff).

So, the relationship between Abraham and Sarah seems to have had at least these components: A wife not afraid to speak her mind; a wife who was willing to abide by her husband's decisions; a husband who made decisions and who made those decisions based on the will of God; and a husband who was willing to take responsibility for his decisions. It will, of course, be up to each individual family to determine how all of this would apply to their circumstances, but it is hoped that this will apply to every family in some way.

It seems appropriate at this point to remind ourselves about our Lord's concept of greatness. According to Him, the spotlight may not always shine on those who truly are great.

> But Jesus called them to Himself and said, 'You know that the rulers of the Gentiles lord it over them, and those who are great exercise authority over them. Yet it shall not be so among you; but whoever desires to become great among you, let him be your servant. And whoever desires to be first among you, let him be your slave-- just as the Son of Man did not come to be served, but to serve, and to give His life a ransom for many' (Matt. 20:25-28).

The familiar story of Dorcas should serve to illustrate this. Where was the call for an apostle when Stephen lost his life? Who was summoned when James was executed? Isn't it interesting that an entire church was affected and that they called for Peter when a *woman* passed from this life? And isn't it of equal interest that "all she did" was to provide clothing for people? The story of Dorcas teaches us that humble and often unnoticed service is what is truly great.

What about Timothy's mother and grandmother? Was it a "small" thing to help him develop his own faith? Were they some of the first in a long line of mothers and grandmothers who tried to control a squirming child during a period of worship and/or Bible study? If so, look at what came of their efforts!

Exactly what honor is there in being a woman; especially one who has chosen to devote herself to being a wife and a mother? I used to ask myself that question a lot. My own mother gave up a career in education in order to devote her time to trying to rear me. It was not until my wife and I had our children that I began to figure out why my mother made that choice.

After much discussion and prayer, my wife made the same choice as my mother had made. In reality, it would be more accurate to say that my wife and I *together* made the choice for her to be a stay-at-home mother.

I will never be able to adequately express my gratitude for the fact that our children always had mom there when they needed her (and they needed her much more often than they thought they did). We have never looked back with regret on that decision we made.

I am also thankful that both our daughter and daughter-in-law have made the choice to not let somebody else rear our grandchildren. Each of these ladies has some very special abilities. They are using those abilities to help mold and shape five precious lives. For what it's worth, I think the "women in my life" are pretty special for making the choices they have made.

When one thinks about it, the fact that "Her children rise up and call her blessed; her husband also, and he praises her" (Prov. 31:28) may have been the sweetest music to the ears of the virtuous woman of Proverbs 31. Not much can take the place of the praise of those whom one loves the most.

Many people consider Abraham Lincoln to be one of our nation's greatest presidents. Many have also read his quote: "All that I am or ever hope to be I owe to my angel mother." I'm sure that any mother would love to hear words like these.

Apparently, Abraham Lincoln's relationship with his own wife left a lot to be desired. One can only imagine the relationship (or lack thereof) between Mr. Lincoln and his wife that would cause him to make the following comment when he was nominated for the presidency. According to one report I read, he stood, took his hat in his hand, and quietly said, "I want to share this with the woman who loves me – my mother."

How sad!

It is hoped that all women will appreciate their special place in God's creation. It is also my hope that all of us will realize that and will live so as to receive a commendation that far surpasses any other: "...Well done, good and faithful servant..." (Matt. 25:21 & 23).

He's No Joke

5

He's No Joke

A few years ago, Reba McEntire wrote and recorded the song, "The Greatest Man I Never Knew." We offer the words to that song as a sobering introduction to a discussion of one of the most important roles any human is asked to assume:

> The greatest man I never knew
>   Lived just down the hall
> And everyday we said hello
>   But never touched at all.
> He was in his paper;
>   I was in my room.
> How was I to know he thought I hung the moon?
> The greatest man I never knew
>   Came home late every night.
> He never had too much to say;
>   Too much was on his mind.
> I never really knew him
>   And now it seems so sad.
> Everything he gave to us took all he had.
> Then the days turned into years
>   And the memories to black and white.

He grew cold like an old winter wind
   Blowing across my life.
The greatest words I never heard
   I guess I'll never hear.
The man I thought would never die
   S'been dead almost a year.
He was good at business
   But there was business left to do.
He never said he loved me.
   Guess he thought I knew.

I wonder how many father-child relationships that song describes. I wonder how many wives and children in families feel as though they really do not know much about "the man of the house." Does he just go off and disappear for a few hours? Does his family know about the work he does to help provide for them? Do those who wear his name know about his background and the background of that name? What "makes him tick?" What are his true feelings about things?

The man who wears the dual role in many families of husband and father may be one of the most misunderstood and underappreciated of God's creation. Husbands and fathers are increasingly portrayed in the modern media as some sort of simple-minded, bumbling, incompetent idiot who is really unaware of what is going on in his family, at work, or in the world in general.

However, the Bible would inform us very clearly that, in God's estimation, the role of husband and/or father **is no joke**. It is a very serious matter and one to which more attention needs to be given than will be possible in this chapter.

Sadly, the Bible contains some information about men who could be considered as great by many standards, but who made some glaring mistakes either as husbands, fathers, or both. Many such examples could be used, but we will look briefly at five.

Eli could be seen as the first in a line of "preachers" whose kids went bad. The despicable behavior of his sons is spelled out in almost too graphic detail in 1 Sam. 2:12ff. A major cause of the problem and the thing that incurred the anger of Jehovah was "...(Eli's) sons made themselves vile, and he did not restrain them" (1 Sam. 3:13).

Eli was invaluable in young Samuel's training, but he "lost" his own sons. Do you know any preachers who can relate to this? Do you know any executives, doctors, etc. who can likewise relate?

Apparently, something was amiss in the relationship between **Samuel** and his sons as well. We will not take the space here to try to discuss Samuel's very important role in the history of God's people. Suffice it to say that, in many ways, he needs to be considered as one of the major people of the Old Testament.

However, there is at least one dent in his armor. Most of us are familiar with the demand made by the children of Israel for a king. The most well known reason for this demand is that the people of Israel wanted to be like other nations (cf. 1 Sam. 8:5). This is not the only reason given.

The same verse that gives us that information also states that the elders of Israel told Samuel, "...Look, you are old, and your sons to do not walk in your ways..." What does that mean? In what ways did they not follow Samuel's example? Was it a matter of administrative style, dress, or personality?

Unfortunately, the answer to those questions is much more serious than any of those things we have suggested. Verse 3 of the same chapter informs us, "But his sons did not walk in his ways; they turned aside after dishonest gain, took bribes, and perverted justice."

If one will read the material found in Matt. 27:17-26, he will read about another "great" man who was, in actuality, a failure. This man would not be considered great as a religious leader, but **Pilate** was, indeed, considered by the people of his day as great in other ways.

Pilate knew the Jews' reason for bringing our Lord to him was not valid. The record states, "For he knew that they had handed Him over because of envy" (v. 18). It will be remembered that Pilate's wife also advised him that Jesus was just and that Pilate should not get involved in this matter cf. (v. 19).

However, it appears to me that Pilate was more concerned about popular opinion and/or his position than he was in doing what he knew to be right. His standing with "the people" seems to have meant more to him than his relationship with his wife.

Pilate's (in)action may have played a role in keeping his family in a position of prominence, but a terrible price was paid for that. Neither his wife nor any other member of his family could ever look up to him as a man who stood on principles.

Two Bible characters have at least one thing in common. **Adam** and **Ananias** may be separated by many centuries, but they exhibit a trait that is still seen all too often today. Each of them failed to take the lead spiritually when it was really important to do so.

Ananias may, in fact, have taken the lead in the deception recorded in Acts 5. While Adam was not the one who took the lead in the events recorded in Genesis 3, he certainly did nothing to exert his leadership and stop the unfortunate chain of events. Much discussion has been done about the meaning of Genesis 3:6 and the meaning of the statement that "...(Eve) also gave to her husband **with her**, and he ate" (emphasis added).

Does that mean that Adam was with her during this whole ordeal? If so, why did he not put a stop to something he knew to be contrary to God's will? Along with being the first man, was he also the first man to fail to be the spiritual leader in his home?

God's word is clear about the responsibilities of the husbands and fathers. It teaches repeatedly and in a variety of places that a married man's primary earthly relationship is to his wife.

Far too many men have failed to realize that. Some think that they must still put their parents' needs, desires, and wishes ahead of their mates. It is true that we have responsibilities toward our parents at every stage of their (and our) lives. 1 Timothy 5:8 is often slightly mis-used to prove that husbands and fathers need to "provide for their own" wives and children. This is true, but, when the verse is read in its context, it will be seen that it deals primarily with the care of widows.

I find four words in Mark 1:20 very interesting and informative. Without these four words, one would get the idea that James and John left their father to fend for himself when they answered Jesus' invitation to follow Him. Look at the verse in its entirety and decide for yourself how important the four words I've chosen to emphasize are: "And immediately He called them, and they left their father Zebedee in the boat **with the hired servants**, and went after Him." It doesn't appear to be the case that Zebedee was totally abandoned.

The same book informs us of a confrontation that Jesus had with some of the Jews. During this particular confrontation, our Lord told these people "...All too well you reject the commandment of God, that you may keep your tradition" (Mark 7:9).

Interestingly enough the specific example He gave concerning this was a "loophole" they had devised to allow them to ignore the command to honor their parents. Our Lord was then, and still is, concerned about the treatment of our parents, but His Word still has the admonition **three times** that we are to "leave" them and "cleave" to our wives (cf. Gen. 2:24; Matt. 19:5; Eph. 5:31). We can be sure that "leave" does not mean "abandon," but we can be just as certain that it does not mean to put them ahead of the wife.

How often do you see families torn apart because one of the spouses puts the interests, perceived needs, and desires of the children ahead of his or her mate? We plan to discuss the very important role that parents are to play in later material, but this is not a marriage partner's primary role. It is unhealthy, not to mention unscriptural, for children to feel as though they are the most important members of the family.

They need to see that dad and mom love each other more than they love them. In this, as well as in so many other matters, the fathers need to take the lead.

It is a sad home wherein the father makes sure that presents are bought in abundance for children, but the wife's birthday, the couple's anniversary, and other important occasions come and go without so much as a mention. It is equally sad when the father has time for every ballgame and all the other activities in which the children are involved, while he never takes the time to explore and nurture his wife's interests.

Children are important, but like parents, they are not a husband's first concern. He should put first (on earth) his relationship with the one who gave up a great deal of her autonomy and chose to wear his name.

A couple of other things vie for our time, attention, and energy. All of us realize that work is commanded by God. In so many ways, He informs us that He expects us to work.

However, the boss is not more important than the spouse. A lot of men seem to want to be defined by what they *do*. They seem to think that their identity is only that of being a lawyer, bricklayer, preacher, etc. I picked up this quote somewhere from William L. Phelps who at one time served as president of Yale University: "No man can be considered a success who is a failure in his own home, and no man can be considered a failure who is a success in his own home."

One more group will be considered briefly as competitors for the time, attention, and energy of husbands. Sometimes they are called "buddies;" sometimes they are referred to as "good ole boys;" sometimes just the more generic "friends" is used. Whatever they are called, the fact remains that they are never to be a substitute for, or in competition with, the family.

Agape is, of course, one of the Greek words translated "love" in our New Testaments. It carries with it the meaning of looking out for the interest of the other person and putting them first. It has often been described in terms of being "self-giving" and/or "sacrificial."

This is the word that is used in Ephesians 5:25 wherein we read, "Husbands, love your wives..." As suggested earlier, this verse, including the challenge for husbands to love their wives "...as Christ also loved the church and gave Himself for her," would go a long, long way in providing the model for the model husband.

Such would be the case also with regard to another passage we have already looked at. 1 Peter 3:7 instructs husbands to dwell with their wives "...with understanding..." Some of the best training one of God's servants ever received is recorded in Ezekiel 3:14-15. In this passage, Ezekiel was taken to live among those to whom he would be delivering God's message. In the words of verse 15, he "...sat where they sat, and remained there astonished among them seven days."

Maybe husbands could learn a lesson here. Maybe we need to try really hard to sit where our wives sit; to see things from her perspective. This would involve much more communication than what presently goes on in far too many families.

In this same verse (1 Peter 3:7), husbands are told to "...give honor to the wife, as to the weaker vessel..." The literal meaning of "showing honor" is "bestowing value."

Husbands need to show their wives how valuable she is to him. They do not need to be like the fellow who was said to have taken his wife to a psychiatrist because she was constantly depressed. In a very short time the doctor figured out where the problem was. He told the man that the treatment he prescribed was very simple. He went over to the man's wife, grabbed her in his arms and gave her a big kiss. He then stepped back and looked at the woman's glowing smile. Turning to the husband, he said, "See! That's all she needs to put new life back into her." Without expression, the husband replied, "O.K., Doc, I golf on Monday, Wednesdays, and Fridays, but I can have her here on Tuesdays and Thursdays." I think he missed the point!

The humorist, Will Rogers, found a unique way to honor his wife. According to one account I read, he was asked to perform at some sort of charity event, but his wife was not invited. Upon his return to his home, he sent the organizers of the event a bill for his services. They, in turn, sent word to him that his services were to have been donated. His reply was to the effect that, if his wife was not invited, he considered it work and he still expected payment. Again, according to the account I read, he received it!

In Colossians 3:19, husbands are told to "...love your wives, and do not be bitter toward them." The English Standard Version reads, "do not be harsh toward them." The original language suggests anything that would cut or prick.

Husbands do not need to cut their wives down or say hurtful things to them even in jest. I cringe every time I hear a wife referred to as "the old ball and chain" or "the old lady." Our buddies might be able to handle unflattering comments about weight or gray hair, but "the weaker vessel" might not be as able to deal with them.

There seems to be a "tie-in" with the man's role as a father. The Holy Spirit used Paul to instruct fathers to "…not provoke your children to wrath" (Eph. 6:4). One translation of this phrase renders it "do not exasperate your children."

Children can be provoked to anger and/or exasperated in a number of ways. Some dads do this by constantly jabbing, poking fun, criticizing, etc. Others do this by not listening or by showing favoritism. I would suggest that all fathers who find themselves doing any of these things need to quit, *and they need to quit right now!*

It is interesting that the last verse of the Old Testament gives the following as one of the roles of John the baptist (referred to as Elijah here): "He shall turn the hearts of the fathers to the children, and the hearts of the children to their fathers, lest I come and strike the earth with a curse" (Malachi 4:6).

We live in a society that desperately needs that. Some fathers are no longer a part of the family due to divorce and/or desertion. Some are too busy pursuing a career, participating in recreational activities, etc. to be effective fathers (or husbands). Others have just abdicated their God-given roles.

It is interesting that the English version of the Greek word translated "honor" in 1 Peter 3:7 is *time*. It does not carry with it the meaning of time, but it is an interesting fact nevertheless. It takes time to be an effective husband and father. This also helps to remind us of the uncertainty of time. We would do well to re-read James 4:13ff. and remind ourselves about how brief and uncertain our earthly existence is.

Husbands and fathers need to work to make sure they are not the greatest man their family never knew. They need to ask themselves, *"If I were to die today, would my loved ones know they were my loved ones?"*

"What We Have Here is A Failure to Communicate"

6

"What We Have Here Is A Failure to Communicate"

Strother Martin is not an actor whose name just tumbles off the lips of many people. It probably does not help to provide the additional information that his name was really Strother Martin, Jr. His name is just not very well known.

A picture of Mr. Martin might help some who remember seeing him in a great number of films and television shows of years gone by. More often than not, he appeared in westerns. He usually portrayed some sort of scruffy character.

However, as little known as he was and as "forgettable" as some of his characters were, Strother Martin's character uttered probably one of the most well remembered lines in the movie *Cool Hand Luke*. In fact, it may be one of the most memorable lines in the history of motion pictures.

His character in this movie was that of a captain on a chain gang to which Paul Newman's character, Luke, had been assigned. When he had trouble getting Luke to do what he wanted him to do, he said,

> What we have here is a failure to communicate. Some men you just can't reach, so you get what we had here last week which

the way he wants it. Well, he gets it. And I don't like it any more than you men.

Later in the movie, Newman's character mocks the captain by repeating, "What we have here is a failure to communicate" back to him. The line has, as they say, "gone down in history."

However, the failure to communicate is not just material for a line in a movie. A failure to communicate is a great problem for a lot of families.

In chapters seven, eight, and nine, we intend to devote much time to the parent-child relationship. At that time, we will take yet another look at the sixth chapter of Deuteronomy. In this chapter, we use Deuteronomy six and focus our attention on what it says about communication.

We believe that there is some valuable information in this chapter about the process of communication among all the members of the family. While our focus will be primarily on the parent-child relationship, we hope we can glean some valuable insights that will help us in all of our relationships.

Verse seven of our text is an important verse. In this verse, the children of Israel are given this instruction about the commandments of God:

> You shall teach them diligently to your children, and shall talk of them when you sit in your house, when you walk by the way, when you lie down, and when you rise up.

It appears that there is room in this one verse for at least two types of training and instruction for the children. The first of these is what might be called "formal training."

The phrase "teach them diligently to your children" is translated "impress them on your children" in the NIV. The phrase comes from a Hebrew word that carries with it the concept of sharpening a knife and/or using a whet stone for that purpose.

I once knew a man in Missouri that told me of one of his chores when he was a young boy. There was an elderly uncle who lived with his family. It was the boy's job to shave the elderly gentleman. There were some factors that made this chore a difficult one.

For one thing, the older man did not want to be shaved on a very regular basis. His very tough beard became more and more difficult to shave because of his refusal to be shaved regularly.

Another problem was that took place back in the days of straight razors. As the man related the story to me, a big part of the process when he was a young boy attempting to shave the man was to try to keep the blade sharp. He said, "I'd shave a while and strop a while; shave a while and strop a while."

That, to me, seems to describe the formal training that children need. It cannot be done all the time, but there needs to be time set aside in a setting conducive to learning for the formal teaching of God's Holy Word.

Bible classes, Vacation Bible Schools, and other such events can go a long way in meeting this need. At the same time, they can never substitute for the ones who have been given the primary responsibility for this training; the parents.

Parents need to schedule times at home for the formal training of their children. It could be that this need is met in the evenings as the children are put to bed with a story from God's word. It could be regularly scheduled family devotionals. It could be a lot of things. *It just needs to be!*

The remainder of Deut. 6:7 leaves the door wide open for "teachable moments." It indicates that God's Word can be spoken and taught during the normal course of one's day and life.

Parents need to look for those "teachable moments." They happen with great frequency, but the challenging thing is that, more often than not, they just happen. It is difficult to plan the exact moment when a child will ask a question or make a statement that demands immediate attention. The unexpected question or statement may provide some insight into the child's thinking about God.

We can't always predict when a rainbow will appear after a rain shower, when we will see a "shooting star," or when some other part of God's creation will provide a teachable moment. The only thing I can predict is that there will be many, many such moments during a child's years at home. ***Parents, be on the alert!***

I believe that parents can do more than just being on the alert. I believe that parents who are thinking ahead will, in fact, "stack the deck" to ensure that there will be teachable moments. The events recorded in Joshua 4:1ff are an example of this.

The fourth chapter of Joshua contains the record of God's people finally crossing through the Jordan River and entering the land of promise. Part of this process involved one representative from each of the twelve tribes taking a stone from the river to stack on the soil of the place of their destination.

If somebody is reading this material for the first time, they might wonder, "Why did God give this instruction? What was the purpose of these stones?" One reason, of course, is that these stones were intended to be "a memorial" (v. 7).

However, there was another reason for this action. Consider verse 6: "that this may be a sign among you when your children ask in time to come, saying, 'What do these stones mean to you?'"

I believe that God was, in effect, tapping into the inquisitive minds of young people. He knew that they would want to know what those stones were all about. He also knew this would provide the **parents** with an opportunity to relate what the stones meant **to them**.

Parents today would do well to find ways to follow this teaching. This "stacking the deck" could take a lot of forms. One way my wife and I did this was with regard to where we wanted our children to go to college. We had both gone to a state university, but we wanted our children to go to a Christian university. In fact, we wanted them to go to a particular Christian university. Each time we visited that campus, we would try to bring something back for them. When colleges were discussed, we made sure that this college was prominently involved in the discussion. Can you guess where they went to college?

There are any number of ways to "stack the deck." I would suggest that parents would be well advised to be creative in this and to find ways that fit their own family situations. One size does not fit all.

Deuteronomy 6:20 is a powerful reminder of the need for good family communication and is an indicator of the type of communication that should exist in the family.

When your son asks you in time to come, saying, 'What is the meaning of the testimonies, the statutes, and the judgments which the Lord our God has commanded you?'

God's plan for families includes an atmosphere in which children should not feel intimidated or threatened to the point where they cannot ask any questions. As the verse above demonstrates, they should feel especially free to ask questions about God, His Word, etc.

Parents, grandparents, elders, preachers and/or any adults can learn a valuable lesson from some events recorded in the second chapter of Luke. These events involve Jesus, as a twelve year old boy, being left in Jerusalem by Joseph and Mary as they began their journey back to their home.

When they came back to Jerusalem to look for Him, ...they found Him in the temple, sitting in the midst of the teachers, both listening to them and asking them questions" (Luke 2:46). As much "bad press" as these men will get as the gospel accounts unfold, they are to be commended here for taking the time to engage in conversation with a twelve year old.

The lesson for parents and other adults is fairly simple: **when I am constantly too busy to spend time with young people, I'm just too busy**. There needs to be adequate time and effort spent on good two-way communication.

This may even tie in with the instruction given to fathers in Ephesians 6:4. In this verse, fathers are told, "...do not provoke your children to wrath..." As we have seen, the NIV translates this as "...do not exasperate your children..." Let's take another look at this.

What exasperates you? When you are talking and you realize that somebody is not listening, do you get exasperated? Are you even sometimes tempted to get angry? How about when unrealistic demands are placed on you? How do those situations affect you? Are you frustrated and/or exasperated when there are no clearly defined rules or boundaries?

Do we somehow think that children are that much different from us? We would do well to determine what frustrates, exasperates, and/or angers us. It would be wise to seek to avoid those things as we deal with our children (or any other members of our families for that matter).

In 1983, *Reader's Digest* printed an article I still keep in my files. I know that the material becomes more and more dated with each passing year, but I believe it is just as relevant now as it was then. The article was condensed from a speech prepared and delivered by Myrle Carner, who was, at that time, a police investigator with the Seattle police department and who had served for twenty-three years in law enforcement.

The title of the article was "What Teen-Agers Are Dying to Tell Their Parents." The subtitle was "Six things kids want – and desperately need – from Mom and Dad." The content of the article was based on what young people on their way to juvenile hall or a detention home had actually told the author. In other words, this is "real life" stuff.

Some of the things may surprise some who read them. Here they are, along with some of the commentary given by the author:

'Keep your cool.' The No. 1 thing: Don't lose your temper in a crunch. Kids need the reassurance that comes from controlled responses.

'Show us who's boss.' Most young people want their parents to be strict. They don't want cruelty, but they do want parents who are consistent in discipline. Kids need to know there are consequences for going over the line.

'Remember who you are.' If you are 40, don't act 16. Your kids need somebody to look up to.

'Talk about God.' Many troubled kids are looking for a genuine spiritual dimension in their lives. They are saying, 'We need to believe in something bigger and stronger than ourselves.'

'**Call our bluff.**' Did you know that kids really don't mean everything they say? They want parents who won't be intimidated when they make a threat.

'**Be honest with us.**' Kids want to be told the truth. They know when you're telling it like it is. They know you better than you know yourself, and they'll accept criticism better when it comes from a mother or father who's honest and up-front.

Paul Faulkner writes, in *Achieving Success Without Failing Your Family*, "The best thing I can think of to describe good communication is openness; the child must be willing and able to express his deepest feelings and concerns to the parent; and the parent must be available and discerning in listening and responding to the child" (p. 50). How is this to be done? That is the question that puzzles so many of us.

All of us are aware of the fact that there are barriers to good communication. We may just not be aware of what they are and/or how to deal with them. A list of all the barriers to communication would be rather lengthy. I will leave it for the experts in the field of communication to deal with all of them. I will just list and discuss briefly some I have noticed over the years.

Physical and/or Mental Limitations

In many of the books and articles I've read, there is no mention of the fact that some people are limited either physically or mentally. This is unfortunate. It is not fair to leave the impression that only those with normal physical and mental health can communicate.

There are people with very serious challenges in these areas, but who still can communicate quite well. We just need to be aware that much effort will be necessary in order for these people to communicate effectively and for others to communicate with them. When the appropriate effort is made, great and rewarding results can and do happen!

Filters

One of the fascinating and, at the same time, challenging things about communication is that this process goes through a variety of filters. If one person is doing the speaking, his words first go through the filters of his background, his perceptions, his ethnicity, his age, his understanding, and a host of other things.

When the message is received, it goes through similar "filters" on that end of the conversation. When one adds to all of that, the filters of society, geography and a host of other things, it is little wonder that so many people complain about not being understood and/or in having trouble in understanding.

Allow me to give just one of what could probably be millions of examples. Suppose somebody with a broken heart was trying to break the news to a friend that he or she has a child who is **gay**. Suppose further that the one who receives the information is "from the old school" where that word meant "happy." Can you not see a potential for a "slight" problem in communication here? It could even happen that the heartbroken parent could be congratulated for rearing such a happy and well adjusted child!

Dusting off Your Crystal Ball

A real barrier to communication is erected when one person thinks he or she knows what the other person is thinking, what they are going to say before it is ever said, and/or their emotions. It is hard to tell somebody something when they've already decided for themselves what you have to say and have, in fact, already begun to work on a response.

An example of sorts of this can be seen in the story of Jacob and Esau's meeting after years of separation. These events are recorded in Genesis 32 & 33.

Jacob already had his mind made up about how dreadfully he might be treated and took steps to protect the family members who were most dear to him. As the account unfolds, however, he learned that Esau did not at all have revenge on his mind. Instead of finding himself in a battle with his brother, he found himself in an embrace! (cf. Gen. 33:4).

Instead of dusting off my crystal ball, I need to put it away. Communication would be much more effective.

Playing Dodge Ball

The woman that Jesus met at the well in Samaria was a great dodge ball player. As you read the account of the conversation that Jesus had with her, it is easy to observe all of the efforts she made to change the subject and, in fact, to try to put Jesus on the defensive (cf. John 4).

Dodge ball is still being played and it is not confined to grade school physical education classes. Husbands, wives, parents, children, and all members of any family often try this tactic to keep from really engaging in conversation.

Good communication will involve staying on the subject, not jumping from one subject to another.

Being An Historian

You may have heard about the fellow who was complaining about his wife becoming historical every time there was a disagreement. His friend tried to correct him by saying, "Don't you mean hysterical?" "No," the man replied, "I mean historical. She brings up everything I've ever done wrong in the past!"

Communication will never be what it can be when one or more of the parties involved insist on being "historical." The situation at the time is what needs to be dealt with. The things that took place in the past should have been taken care of in the past. Even if they were not, they do not need to be brought into a current discussion. Resolve the current situation first. Then, maybe something from the past could be fairly dealt with, if there is a need to do so.

Lighting the Fuse

Most of us, especially in family situations, know what issues, words, and/or ideas to avoid. How many conversations have been destroyed because somebody refused to resist the temptation to light the fuse on a firecracker we know will go off?

"Let your speech always be with grace, seasoned with salt..." (Col. 4:6). This admonition leaves little room for something that we know will ignite a situation.

"It Ain't Me, Babe"

Sonny and Cher weren't the only ones to use those words. At least, they weren't the only ones to have that idea.

The blame game has destroyed many conversations and relationships and needs to be avoided. This game has been around for a long time, hasn't it? In the garden, Adam blamed Eve (and God) and Eve blamed the serpent.

It cannot possibly be true that one person is always to blame in every situation where there is a disagreement. Sometimes, (many times) I need to realize that I am the one who is at fault and I need to do what I can to rectify the situation.

Identifying problems may go some distance in solving them, but we wouldn't go to a doctor who only was interested in diagnosing physical problems. We would want to go to one who could point us to a solution.

What follows in this discussion are some principles I believe will help families, churches, communities, as all of us seek to communicate more effectively.

2 Are More Than 1

Now that you know that I am a real math expert, let me explain what I mean by that. The thought is certainly not original with me that

God gave us two ears and one mouth. Maybe He was trying to tell us something.

Far too many people think they are communicating only when they are talking. This is far from the truth. Good communication will involve listening as well; maybe a lot more listening than talking.

I cannot count the number of times people have come into my office or home or asked me to come to their home because they wanted me to help them with a problem they were having. In a great number of these cases, I've sat and listened for quite a long period of time. When the person is through talking, he or she will often say, "Thank you. You've helped me so much."

What did I do? I didn't give any great words of advice. I didn't come up with a solution for what they were dealing with. I didn't *do* anything except **listen**.

Learn to listen. You may surprise yourself at how effective you have become as a communicator. We need to remember that we are instructed, "...let every man be swift to hear, slow to speak..." (James 1:19).

Repeatedly, during His earthly ministry, Jesus told the Jews, "You say..." (cf. Matt. 15:5, 16:2, etc.). To be sure, He was usually in the process of correcting some of their misunderstandings or misinterpretation of scripture. At the same time, though, He was letting them know He had been *listening* to what they had been saying.

The Eyes Have it

In some meetings where votes are taken, the ayes have it. In communication, often the *eyes* have it.

Luke 7:13 is just one example of this. This verse is part of the account of the widow from Nain who had just lost her son to death. This verse states, "When the Lord saw her, He had compassion on her and said to her, 'Do not weep.'"

A very important principle of communication is found here and elsewhere in Jesus' ministry. *Jesus observed people.*

Those who are experts in the field of communication inform us that we listen as much with our eyes as we do with our ears. Whether it is family members or others we are talking about, we need to *look at them* when they are speaking to us and when we are speaking to them.

Honesty Does Not Have to be Brutal

"Let me be brutally honest."

That sentence usually precedes something that is very unpleasant. Hurt feelings, broken hearts, and/or broken relationships have been some of the results of somebody being "brutally honest."

Honesty, or truth, is vital to our relationship with God. We, of course, must obey and live by the truth. We must also speak the truth.

However, the Bible also speaks of "...speaking the truth **in love**..." (Eph. 4:15, emphasis added). *How* we say something can have as great an impact as *what* we say.

I have a friend with whom I used to work at church camp each summer. I've heard him do a little "comedy routine" for the campers many times. Part of that routine involved a blind date that a buddy of his supposedly fixed him up with.

According to the story, when he stopped by the girl's house, she was very, very overweight. As they were riding along in the car, he said he remembered that his mother always told him to try to find something nice to say about everybody. He says he turned to the girl and said, "You don't sweat much for a fat girl, do you?"

I don't know if that qualifies as "brutally honest," but it was brutal and it was honest. Let's see if we can't do a better job than that.

Replace the Television with the Dinner Table

There is an interesting account in 1 Samuel 20:25ff. Actually these verses pick up the story of Saul's animosity toward David and his plans to eliminate this threat to his power and popularity. The story also involves the loyalty that Jonathan demonstrated to his friend, David.

Saul was not sure what was going on, but he knew something was different as they sat down to eat because "...David's place was empty" (1 Sam. 20:25 & 27). Imagine that; somebody being missed at a meal because they were not sitting in their usual place!

Modern families eat on the run and often eat separately. If, on a rare evening, all of the family members find themselves at home, they might be found eating while watching television or fiddling with some electronic device.

There is a real need in our society to use the dinner table for something other than a nice piece of furniture to be admired. There is a need for the family to sit as a unit around the table with no distractions and share their days and their lives.

Some of the best memories I have of the house in which I was reared and, then later, of the houses in which our children were reared involve eating together. The food was always good, but one can get at least a decent meal at a lot of places.

What is memorable and what is missed now that our children are no longer at home and my parents have passed away is the time we had as a family to share more than a meal. *We got to share in each other's lives.*

Is communication really all that important? Specifically, is communication with our children important?

Before you answer that question, please read the following letter that appeared in an Ann Landers column a number of years ago:

Dear Ann Landers,

I am writing from behind bars. The charge? A felony – child molesting. Not a pleasant subject, I realize, but this letter is not being written to be pleasant or to gain sympathy. You've never seen me in the parks or near playgrounds looking for victims. I don't play ball and I don't give out candy. I don't leer at children or stare at them, yet I've never lacked for victims. I've held several positions of responsibility working with the public. You've probably met me and liked me. Your children have learned that I can fix a bike and will talk to them when no one else has time to listen. When Mom was too busy or Dad was too tired, they came to me. I know more about your children's teachers and their school problems than you because they knew I was interested. The two little girls I molested can never regain what was taken away from them and I will spend five years in prison. I was molested as a child and feel certain that at least two of my victims will grow up to be molesters. I am sick at heart, but the damage is done and I can't undo it.

The next time your child has something to tell you, don't be too busy to listen. Ask yourself, 'If I won't listen, who will?'

God's Parenting Manual

7

God's Parenting Manual

Young men have strong passions and tend to gratify them indiscriminately...They are changeable and fickle in their desires, which are violent while they last, but quickly over... They think they know everything, and are always quite sure about it; this, in fact is why they overdo everything. (Aristotle; 384-322 B.C.)

> Children now live in luxury, they have bad manners, contempt for authority; they show disrespect for elders and love to chatter in place of exercise. Children are now tyrants of the household. They no longer rise when an elder enters the room and they contradict their parents. They chatter before company and gobble up the food at the table; they cross their legs and tyrannize their teachers. (Socrates; 470-399 B.C.)
>
> I see no hope for the future of our people if they are dependent on the frivolous youth of today, for certainly all youth are reckless beyond words...When I was a boy, we were taught to be discreet and respectful of elders, but the present youth are exceedingly wise and impatient of restraint. (Hesoid; 8th century B.C.)

If the quotations reproduced above are reflective of anything, they are reflective of the fact that the so called "generation gap" is not a new phenomenon. Apparently, there has been some distance between the generations for quite some time.

With the popularity of the concept of a generation gap a number of years ago, there was also a growing popularity in new and innovative ways for parents to "relate to" their children. Out were the days of discipline and instruction and in were the days of understanding and open-mindedness.

In the "post-modern" world of today where there are no absolutes, why should anybody accept the old-fashioned idea that parents were actually responsible for providing their children with a moral compass? Shouldn't the children be allowed, even encouraged, to "do their own thing?"

Whatever one's view of parenting is, all will agree that time seems to move at two different speeds at various stages during the process. For the young couple trying to rear small children, it seems at times like the process will never end. For those of us who are now looking back on the time when our children were at home, it seems as though it only lasted for a minute or two.

In 1986, the following material appeared in the Ann Landers column. It illustrates this point well.

Wet Oatmeal Kisses

The baby is teething. The children are fighting. Your husband just called and said, 'Eat dinner without me.'

One of these days you'll explode and shout to the kids, 'Why don't you grow up and act your age!' And they will.

Or: 'You guys get outside and find yourselves something to do. And don't slam the door!' And they don't.

You'll straighten their bedrooms all neat and tidy – toys displayed on the shelf, hangers in the closet, animals caged.

You'll yell, 'Now I want it to stay this way!' And it will.

You will prepare a perfect dinner with a salad that hasn't had all the olives picked out and a cake with no finger traces in the icing and you'll say: 'Now THIS is a meal for company.' And you will eat it alone.

You'll yell, 'I want complete privacy on the phone. No scream-ing. Do you hear me?' And no one will answer.

No more plastic tablecloths stained with spaghetti. No more dandelion bouquets. No more iron-on patches. No more wet, knotted shoelaces, muddy boots or rubber bands for ponytails.

Imagine. A lipstick with a point. No baby sitter for New Year's Eve, washing clothes only once a week, no PTA meetings or silly school plays where your child is a tree. No carpool, blaring ste-reos or forgotten lunch money.

No more Christmas presents made of library paste and tooth-picks. No wet oatmeal kisses. No more tooth fairy. No more gig-gles in the dark, scraped knees to kiss or sticky fingers to clean. Only a voice asking: 'Why don't you grow up?"

And the silence echoes: 'I did.'

I have no way of providing adequate information concerning the number of books, articles, etc. that have been written on the subject of parenting. The material written here is not intended to necessarily add any information to that abundance of information.

It is intended to point people to, and comment on, what I believe is the best "parenting manual" ever produced. The specific material we intend to consider is found in the sixth chapter of Deuteronomy.

This particular scripture is, like the rest of God's Word, a wonderful example of balance. Balance is a theme that is demonstrated repeat-edly as we read the Bible. Just a couple of examples should suffice to illustrate this.

The first one that may come to mind is that acceptable worship is to be "...in spirit and in truth" (John 4:24). We also remember the words of Romans 11:22 which speak of "...the goodness and severity of God..."

Amazingly, some modern thinking has "come around" to the idea that proper parenting should follow a balanced approach. I would suggest that this thinking is getting close to saying that parents should follow a *scriptural* approach; even though many of these experts would not want to use that term at all.

On October 19, 1994, an article appeared in the *St. Louis Post* entitled "Authoritative: The Best Style of Parenting." As I read the article, I was fascinated by its contents. It seemed to me that our modern thinking was finally beginning to "catch up" with some instructions given through Moses to the children of Israel a long, long time ago.

Space will not permit the reproduction of the article here, but we will try to summarize *very briefly* its contents. The thrust of the article was a comparison of four different styles of parenting.

The first style was what the authors called the **authoritarian style of parenting**. Archie Bunker was used as the "model" for this style of parenting in which the parents are "...stern and controlling..." This style of parenting "...is characterized by a 'because-I-say-so' attitude."

The authors also discussed the **indulgent parenting style**. One expert was quoted as calling this "The Happiness Trap." "This parent can't stand to have her child unhappy...She needs to always have her child feel loving toward her." This type of parent is characterized as being "...wishy-washy, either inconsistent or non-existent in limit setting, often letting the child set the limits."

Disengaged parenting was also looked upon by the authors as being far from the best style of parenting. This parent lets others set the rules and limits. Many times, somebody else is rearing the children while this type of parent is pursuing a career.

The authors wrote approvingly of **the authoritative style of parenting**. In this style of parenting, there definitely are rules and limits, but these rules and limits are often explained. They may even change at various stages in the lives of the children and other family members.

One expert suggested, "Watch a rerun of 'The Cosby Show' and you're seeing it in action...Cosby is warm, affectionate and relatively strict, but it's a strictness that is reasoned and reasonable, based on the belief that what children need from their parents is guidance and training." (While Mr. Cosby's personal life has been scrutinized a lot in recent years, the authors of the newspaper article were commenting on the character he portrayed in the television series.)

It almost appears as if we have returned to the sixth chapter of Deuteronomy. What follows will be a look at its contents and an examination of how this material can still be a guide for parents today. I believe this to be true even after all these years and in spite of the fact that we are under a different covenant.

I am well aware of the fact that many who would write material based on Deuteronomy 6 would begin a discussion of parenting in verse seven wherein the following is written concerning the commandments of God: "You shall teach them diligently to your children, and shall talk of them when you sit in your house, when you walk by the way, when you lie down, and when you rise up."

However, it is my firm conviction that the "parenting advice" found in this remarkable chapter does not begin at verse seven. There is some challenging and informative material in the first six verses that needs to be seriously considered before we enter into a discussion of verse seven.

Repeatedly, in verses one through six of the sixth chapter of Deuteronomy, it is evident that it is the *adults* to whom the words are addressed. In these verses, they are reminded again and again about the importance of learning and obeying the commandments of God.

Just prior to verse seven, we read the words that comprise a portion of what is still known as the Shema, a daily prayer that was (is) to be uttered by every practicing Jew:

Hear, O Israel: The Lord our God, the Lord is one! You shall love the Lord your God with all your heart, with all your soul, and with all your strength. And these words which I command you today shall be in your heart.

One of the "rules" of learning is that the teacher cannot teach what he or she does not know. Correspondingly, one of the "rules" of leadership is that a leader cannot expect people to follow where he or she is unwilling to go.

It appears to be very clear that, before one would attempt to teach his or her children God's way, he or she must know that way and be a practitioner thereof. We would find this to be true as we study Deuteronomy six and as we look at many of the families around us.

The "do as I say and not as I do" method of child-rearing will rarely produce the results that the parents at least give lip-service to.

Maybe the concept of "lip service" is part of the problem. It could well be that some parents only verbalize the sentiment that they want their children to be faithful Christians. The reality may be something else entirely. In reality, the parents may have a greater desire for their children to be financially successful, popular with one or more segments of society, or any number of other things that have nothing to do with spirituality.

Please notice again that *it is the parents who are the ones who are being addressed.* It seems to me that the very best parenting "style" would start with parents who, themselves, love the Lord with all of their being.

Read verse seven again. Does it say that the parents are to talk **only** to their children about the commandments of God? Does the verse not indicate that talking about God's commandments should be a part of the parents' everyday life?

What do your children hear you talking about during the normal course of your day? Do they know what your favorite sports teams are? Do they know what your favorite foods are? Do they know what style of clothing or type of automobile you prefer? *Do they not know these things about you, and many more, at least in part because they hear you talking about them?*

Most people have a habit of talking about things that really interest them. They talk of these things during the normal course of a day – and a life.

Parents need to ask themselves if their children have ever heard them talk to anybody else about our Father, our Savior, His church, His teachings, and a myriad of other matters. If you have children, why not ask yourself, "What *do* my kids hear me talking about?"

Verses eight and nine need to be considered in this context.

You shall bind them as a sign on your hand, and they shall be as frontlets between your eyes. You shall write them on the doorposts of your house and on your gates (Deut. 6:8-9).

When we remember our Lord's scorching denunciation of some of the religious leaders of His day, we need to be aware of the fact that people can, and often do, let ceremony substitute for devotion. It is interesting that, one of the denunciations spoken by Jesus involved the wearing of the very things God had commanded in Deut. 6:8-9. Not only were the scribes and Pharisees wearing them, but they had made them large in order that everybody could see that they were wearing them. At the same time, they were not keeping the very law they were supposedly upholding and following (cf. Matt. 23:1ff).

Ceremony had replaced devotion in their lives. The same can happen to us.

If we just "go to church" and do not worship, we may be in the same boat they were in. If the Bible becomes only a decoration in our home and is not the volume that contains the truths by which we live, we are in danger. Do I spend more energy participating in the "worship wars" of our day or in offering to God my very best as I worship?

The list could go on and on. Suffice it to say that the Jews may not have been the last people to substitute ceremony for devotion. Remember, our children are watching – and learning.

Could our children be learning from us that evangelism is only the preacher's job? Could they be learning from the priorities they observe us having that school work, sporting events, etc. are much more important than worshiping God? Could they be "watching" the "sermons" we preach with our lives and believe that it is more important to be popular than spiritual? When income tax time rolls around or they hear us discussing business deals, do they learn that it is acceptable to lie, cheat, and/or steal "just a little?"

There is some fascinating material in Deuteronomy 6 about the relative importance of material things.

So it shall be, when the Lord your God brings you into the land of which He swore to your fathers, to Abraham, Isaac, and Jacob, to give you large and beautiful cities which you did not build, houses full of all good things, which you did not fill, hewn-out wells which you did not dig, vineyards and olive trees which you did not plant--when you have eaten and are full-- then beware, lest you forget the Lord who brought you out of the land of Egypt, from the house of bondage.

Every time I read these words, I think of my generation. I am one of those "baby boomers" we hear so much about. I have no idea what it must have been like to have lived through The Great Depression.

However, my parents knew from their own personal experience exactly what it was like. They also knew what it was like to grow up in families where every member had to pull his or her weight in order for the family just to survive.

When I came along, my father had gone to work in an electrical plant. I was given chores to do and was expected to do them. At the same time, my family's survival did not depend on the faithful execution of those chores (though at times I wondered if *my* survival did!).

In my mind, my generation and the generations that have followed us are much like the children of Israel when they went into the land of promise. We are the beneficiaries of the hard work and sacrifice of others. We often fail to be as thankful to them as we should.

We also often fail to be as thankful to God as we should. In fact, our material blessings may cause us to forget God. Many are so blessed materially that they seem to think that they do not need God.

There is an interesting passage in the eighth chapter of Deuteronomy. In this passage, there is a warning similar to the one we find in Deuteronomy six. The children of Israel are once again warned not to let affluence cause them to forget God or his commandments.

Along with that warning, we find these words:

then you say in your heart, 'My power and the might of my hand have gained me this wealth.' And you shall remember the Lord your God, for ***it is He who gives you power to get wealth***, that He may establish His covenant which He swore to your fathers, as it is this day (Deut. 8:17-18, emphasis added).

This seems to be an appropriate place to suggest another warning for parents, for elders, for preachers, and for all of us. Some of us have fallen into the trap of believing that material success (or other types of success that deal with growing numbers) are evidence that God is with us and is pleased with what we are doing.

We are not the first and we will probably not be the last to think this way. We would do well to remember that Micah was trying to correct this idea. In the midst of a searing denunciation and dire warning, he wrote this of the leaders of Jerusalem:

Her heads judge for a bribe, Her priests teach for pay, and her prophets divine for money. Yet they lean on the Lord and say, 'is not the Lord among us? No harm can come upon us (Micah 3:11).

I often wonder how "blessed" we really are to live in an affluent society. Most of us would not agree at all that we are rich.

However, two short-term mission trips to India were enough to convince me that I am, in fact, rich. I would argue that, even those in our society who may find themselves living below the "poverty line" are rich when compared to millions of people in other nations.

Let me share with you something I find to be very interesting. As I think of my experience in India, one thing stands out in my mind. I never remember one of those "unfortunate people" ever complaining – about anything!

However, in our nation where we live in air conditioned and heated houses, drive cars with lots of "bells and whistles," have money in the bank, and have so many things that people in other nations cannot even dream of having, depression is almost a way of life. There must be something that is much more important than money and things.

A Christian university did a study a number of years ago. They were trying to determine why young people either remained faithful or left the church after they graduated from high school. They found a number of positive factors that contributed to the faithfulness of these young people. Among the positive factors were the parents' spiritual commitment, good family communication, and church attendance (I guess "dragging the kids to church" was not such a bad idea after all!).

Interestingly enough, there was one negative factor that far exceeded all others in its influence. That factor was *family income*. The study showed that the more affluent the family was, the less willing a young person was to rely on Christ.

Parents who lived by the Old Testament were instructed about the proper priorities. Parents who follow the teaching of Christ would be well advised to remember His comment on priorities as recorded in Matthew 6. After discussing some of the material needs we all have and the fact that some people spend an inordinate amount of time pursuing these things, He said, "But seek first the kingdom of God and His righteousness, and all these things will be added to you" (v. 33).

We hope to enter into a discussion of various ways to teach children in the next chapter, but the intent of this chapter has been to try to suggest the importance of the parents' commitment to God and the need to set the proper example for the children.

Harry and Sandy Chapin tried to convey this same message in the song "Cat's in the Cradle."

My child arrived just the other day;
    he came to the world in the usual way.
But there were planes to catch and bills to pay.
    He learned to walk while I was away.
And he was talkin' 'fore I knew it. And as he grew he'd say,
    "I'm gonna be like you, Dad. You know I'm gonna be like you."
My son turned ten just the other day;
    He said, "Thanks for the ball, Dad. Come on, let's play.
Can you teach me to throw?" I said, "Not today.
    I've got a lot to do." He said, "That's okay."
And he walked away, but his smile never dimmed. It said,
    "I'm gonna be like him, yeah. You know I'm gonna be like him."
And the cat's in the cradle and the silver spoon,
    little boy blue and the man in the moon.

"When you comin' home, Dad?" "I don't know when,
   but we'll have a good time then, Son
You know we'll have a good time then."
Well he came home from college just the other day,
   so much like a man I just had to say,
"Son I'm proud of you. Can you sit for a while?"
   He shook his head and he said with a smile,
"What I'd really like, Dad, is to borrow the car keys.
   See you later. Can I have them, please?"
I've long since retired, my son's moved away.
   I called him up just the other day.
I said, "I'd like to see you if you don't mind."
   He said, "I'd love to, Dad, if I can find the time.
You see, my new job's a hassle and the kids have the flu,
   but it's sure nice talkin' to you, Dad. It's been sure nice talkin'
to you."
And as I hung up the phone it occurred to me,
   he'd grown up just like me. My boy was just like me.
And the cat's in the cradle and the silver spoon,
   little boy blue and man in the moon.
"When you comin' home, son?" "I don't know when,
   but we'll have a good time then, Dad.
We're gonna have a good time then."

Parenting Pointers From A Non-Parenting Passage

8

Parenting Pointers From A Non-Parenting Passage

The book of Hebrews is not normally considered as a guide for parenting. Hebrews is a valuable storehouse of treasures for the student of God's Word in so many ways. For those who need to be reminded of the greatness of God, the superiority of the New Testament dispensation, and a host of other encouraging subjects, the book of Hebrews is invaluable. Hebrews can help the student understand many of the "shadows" found in the Old Testament and how they became a reality in the New Testament.

It is of interest that one can find in this book the answer to the seemingly age old question about the thief on the cross and how he was saved without any record of him being baptized. As one reads the information contained in chapter nine and verses sixteen and seventeen, the answer becomes obvious. Our Lord's "will" did not go into effect until after His death. He could, and did, grant pardon without evidence of baptism *before* His death. For those of us on this side of the cross, however, we must comply with the conditions set forth in His "will."

One subject that is rarely discussed with regard to the book of Hebrews is that of parenting. There is, it seems to me, a great passage on this subject in this great book. To be sure, the subject being discussed is *not* our role as parents, but how God deals with His children.

However, in the course of that discussion , there are some great pointers for parents. This is especially true when it comes to the subject of **discipline**.

The passage under consideration is Hebrews 12:5-11. In the midst of a discussion intended to encourage Christians to not become discouraged because of some of the things they are experiencing, we read the following:

> And you have forgotten the exhortation which speaks to you as to sons: '*My son, do not despise the chastening of the* LORD, *Nor be discouraged when you are rebuked by Him; For whom the* LORD *loves He chastens, And scourges every son whom He receives.*'
>
> If you endure chastening, God deals with you as with sons; for what son is there whom a father does not chasten? But if you are without chastening, of which all have become partakers, then you are illegitimate and not sons. Furthermore, we have had human fathers who corrected *us,* and we paid *them* respect. Shall we not much more readily be in subjection to the Father of spirits and live? For they indeed for a few days chastened *us* as seemed *best* to them, but He for *our* profit, that *we* may be partakers of His holiness. Now no chastening seems to be joyful for the present, but painful; nevertheless, afterward it yields the peaceable fruit of righteousness to those who have been trained by it.

What is discipline? According to one website I consulted the United States Marine Corps defines discipline as follows:

> Discipline is the instant willingness and obedience to all orders, respect for authority, self-reliance and teamwork. The ability

to do the right thing even when no one is watching or suffer the consequences of guilt which produces pain in our bodies, through pain comes discipline.

While I am a little concerned about the sentence structure (or lack of it) in the above quotation, I am more intrigued by the relationship between pain and discipline. It seems that the above definition reinforces what many already believe about discipline; the only time a parent disciplines a child is when the parent spanks the child.

Apparently one little girl did not believe this. I found in my files the following actual note written by a little girl to her father. The grammar, spelling, etc. is hers:

> World's gatist father,
> My father is the gratist,
> for you're the best,
> caring, loveing,
> THE BEST!!!!!!
> even when you disaplin me,
> I love you the same,
> Love,
> Holly

If it is true that discipline only takes place when pain is inflicted, one wonders if the term "academic discipline" means "the pain of going to school!" While I am quite sure that many school students would readily agree with that "logic," it is definitely *not* the case.

It will not be the design of this chapter to involve ourselves in a deep word study; either English or Greek words. That can be left to others. There will be some references made to this, but this is not a "word study" chapter.

At the same time, as one consults a dictionary of the English language for the definition of "discipline," he or she will see that training plays a vital role. *Discipline includes, but is not limited to, punishment.*

The remainder of this chapter will consider the text from Hebrews reproduced above (Heb. 12:5-11). An attempt will be made to provide some parenting pointers from the passage. These pointers will specifically focus on the subject of discipline.

Discipline Is Designed To Be Instructive and Destructive

As the term "academic discipline" suggests, there must be some instruction involved in discipline. In fact, in reality, there can be no discipline without instruction.

Even if we were to limit our understanding and definition of discipline to punishment, the one who is being punished would need to know the reason for the punishment? What "rules" did he/she violate? What behavior went beyond the limits? What is acceptable and what is not acceptable?

These, along with many other, questions cannot be answered without *instruction*. There must be time, energy, and interest invested in order to "positively" discipline a child (or one's self for that matter).

At the same time, discipline cannot be all about "positive reinforcement." It most certainly cannot be about never "pulling in the reins" on a child.

A vital part of discipline is getting rid of the behaviors, attitudes, etc. that are unacceptable. It may be helpful to remember the reason for the punishment that God decreed on Eli and his family: "...his sons made themselves vile, and *he did not restrain them*" (1 Sam. 3:13, emphasis added). Does it not seem reasonable that some restraint might have "destroyed" some of that vile behavior?

Discipline is Designed to be Encouraging and Discouraging

It may be that another way to express what was just discussed would be to say that proper discipline is intended to encourage good behavior and discourage bad behavior. While parents cannot perceive their God-given responsibility as merely rewarding a child for proper behavior and punishing that same child for unacceptable behavior, there must be an element of this involved in child-rearing.

It is to be remembered that, when Paul wrote to the church at Rome, he reminded them of "...the goodness and severity of God..." (Rom. 11:22). Positive reinforcement was given to those who were obedient, while punishment was meted out to those who were not.

A parent who *only* encourages when he/she is pleased with a child's behavior is only doing half a job. Likewise the parent who *only* discourages when he/she is not being pleased is doing only half a job. Parents need to encourage *and* discourage – both at the appropriate times.

Discipline is Designed to be Temporary and Permanent
-OR-
Short-Term and Long-Term

I am intrigued by the phrases "...for a few days..." (v. 10) and "...for the present..." (v. 11). In both instances the unpleasant side of discipline is under discussion.

This indicates that the punishment of a child needs to *not* be an ongoing perpetual thing. If such is done in terms of physical punishment, that would be child abuse. If done perpetually in other ways, it would be abuse in another form. Even coaches of athletic teams don't leave a player "in the doghouse" continually.

While the actual punishment of a child should only be temporary, the *effects* are intended to be long-lasting; in fact, *life*-long lasting. Our society is presently paying a huge debt because of the failure on the part of so many parents for so many generations to take the time when needed to discipline their children.

"Chasten your son while there is hope, And do not set your heart on his destruction" (Prov. 19:18).

Discipline is Designed to be Unpleasant and Pleasant

We have already briefly mentioned the positive and not-so-positive aspects of discipline. This particular point is not about positive reinforcement and/or encouragement vs. punishment.

What the point is here is that *at the time*, discipline may not seem to be (and may, in fact *not be*) pleasant. Whether we are talking about the instruction and training involved in discipline or the punishment, this would be true. At the same time, the "end result" of proper discipline is designed to be *very pleasant*.

There must be some attention given to the fact that Hebrews 12:6 suggests two forms of discipline. A word study of the original language would inform us that both *verbal* and *physical* forms of discipline may be employed.

There are two things that need to be kept in mind, regardless of the form of discipline and/or punishment the parent uses. Both would fit under the heading that "the punishment must fit the crime."

What is meant by that is that parents need to take care to not overreact to minor infractions. "Wearing out" a child for something that is not all that big of a deal would not be appropriate.

At the same time, when a child needs to be punished, whatever form of punishment is chosen should be something that "hurts." Some parents seem to model their "punishment" after the behavior of some people who belong to religious groups which observe the season of Lent. They make a mockery of it by giving up something (in the case of those who "observe" Lent) or taking something away (in the case of "punishment) that the person did not care about and was not going to do anyway!

That adult who is a model citizen and a wonderful Christian example did not get that way overnight. Osmosis is not responsible for his or her behavior and lifestyle. It took a lot of what seemed at the time to be very unpleasant things to make this a reality.

"Correct your son, and he will give you rest; Yes, he will give delight to your soul" (Prov. 29:17)

Discipline is Designed to be Motivated by Love

The text says, "For the Lord disciplines *the one He loves...*" (Heb. 12:6, emphasis added). Is parenting frustrating? Are parents capable of "losing their cool?" Without a doubt, the answer to both of those questions is a resounding "Yes!"

At the same time, children need to know that their parents love them. This is almost impossible for a small child to understand, but, with some maturity, there will also be some understanding of this concept.

Telling a child that he or she is loved while the child is going through either the training or punishing part of discipline is not as effective as *demonstrating* love on a regular basis.

Mark it down! Whenever you see a child out of control and suffering no consequences from a parent, you are seeing a child who is not loved by a parent. The parent is *not* looking out for the best interests of the child.

"*He who spares the rod hates his son, But he who loves him disciplines him properly*" (Prov. 13:24).

Discipline is Designed to be a "Respect Earner"

Please consider the weight of these words: "...we have had human fathers who corrected us *and we paid them respect...*" (Heb. 12:9). "Respect" sounds almost like a foreign word in our culture. Where is the respect of earlier generations for our government, law enforcement officials, educators, parents, or *God*?

One reason for the lack of respect so apparent in our day is tied to the lack of any form of discipline; especially punishment. Why do so many people "wink at" the speed limit signs? Is it not because the consequences of their failure to obey the law are not *immediate* and *severe*? How many people would be much more careful about how fast they drove if they knew that their first infraction would result in them permanently losing their license and/or having their vehicle confiscated *on the spot*? (I am not, by the way, endorsing that!)

Where did the idea of "alternative schools" come from? Whatever happened to the days of old when a child forfeited his opportunity for an education because of his misbehavior? Why should a child respect a teacher or an administrator today when he or she will get a diploma regardless of behavior?

Parents, here's another one to "mark down." If you are not demanding respect from your children, *they are laughing at you!* They may not be doing it to your face (though some are bold enough to do so), *but I guarantee that they are doing so with their friends – and sometimes to their preacher (if they have one)!*

Discipline is Designed to be an Inexact "Science"

I find great comfort in the words in Hebrews 12:10 "...as seemed best to them..." What a relief!

As the Holy Spirit inspired these words to be written, He left open the possibility that *earthly* fathers are, in fact, human. While God is perfect in His "parenting" of His children, we cannot be.

This truth should cause us to do a couple of things. First, as important as parenting is, we should feel a sense of relief in knowing that we cannot "make the correct call" all of the time. Parents *will and do* make mistakes.

Secondly, this fact should cause parents to be more open and honest with their children. There are times when a father or mother (or both) would need to sit down with those who are under their care and admit a lack of understanding the entire situation, an overreaction, or any number of other things that caused the parent to fail to handle a particular situation properly.

A parent who is too big to say "I'm sorry" to a child is too little to be entrusted with the training of that child.

So what does an imperfect parent do when a child says something like, "I hate you!" or "You don't love me!" or "As soon as I turn eighteen, I'm oughta here!"? Are parents to always admit that they make mistakes and begin to do whatever is necessary to make the child happy again?

Does a wise parent **beg**? Groveling is unbecoming; especially when a parent does it.

Does the parent **bribe** or **bargain**? Cookies can turn into new cars before we know it.

What about being a **buddy**? While that seems to be a common practice in many families, parents need to recognize that their children already have plenty of buddies. They also need to recognize how ridiculous a parent looks trying to "be" a teen.

Maybe the proper response is to **bend**, but not **break**. Due to the facts that no two situations are alike and that no parent is perfect, a little bending (relaxing) of some rules may be appropriate for a short time. At the same time, parents need to be careful about breaking. Parents need to set definite boundaries that are, themselves, strong. Rules and expectations that are always broken are not strong enough. Along with this, the parents need to be strong enough to make sure those boundaries remain intact. The parents cannot break, even when it is very tempting to do so.

The plural, "parents," keeps being used in this discussion. I realize that every home is not blessed with two parents living under the same roof. Single parents are at a disadvantage *except* in the cases in which the parents, themselves, are in conflict about discipline and/or one parent takes the side of one or more of the children. Have we forgotten the preferential treatment that was much of the cause of the conflict between Jacob and Esau?

Parents need to **parent**. *They* are the adults. *They* need to guide, train, discipline, punish, love, and do everything else involved in rearing children. They do *not* need to look to the educational system, society as a whole, or even the church to do what God has given them the responsibility of doing.

Parents need to **pray**. If there is any endeavor which is more serious and for which most people have less amount of training, I'm unaware of what it would be. Most parents just sort of go by what they liked and did not like about how they were reared. They may buy a few books, attend a class or two, or do some other such things. All parents who are thinking at all should recognize the need for God's help and will spend much time in prayer.

Parents need to **persist**. The old adage informs us that "Rome was not built in a day." Similarly, children are not mushrooms; they do not spring up full-grown overnight. They are more like giant oak trees that grow at slow and, at times, almost imperceptible rates. What "worked" today may be forgotten tomorrow. Parents need to remind themselves that, in spite of what looks like evidence to the contrary, something is "getting through" to those minds and hearts – for good or ill. Hopefully it will be for good.

I don't believe I have ever met anybody who thinks that he or she "has arrived" as a parent. It my prayer that these "parenting pointers" will be useful on the journey.

How Does Our View of God Influence Our Parenting?

9

How Does Our View of God Influence Our Parenting?

love to read and hear about the various views of God that are held and expressed by small children. Some of them are very humorous and some are quite thought provoking. I often wonder if small children might not have some insight into the nature, the heart, and the mind of God that those of us who are older might benefit from.

In *House to House/Heart to Heart* (Vol. 11, No. 1) there were some thoughts that I found interesting. A few of them are reproduced here:

Dear God, I keep waiting for spring, but it never came yet. Don't forget. – Mark

Dear God, You don't have to worry about me. I look both ways. – Dean

Dear God, I think about you sometimes even when I'm not praying. – Elliott

Dear God, I bet it is hard for you to love all of everybody in the whole world. There are only four people in our family and I can never do it.

Dear God, If you watch in church on Sunday, I will show you my new shoes. – Mickey D.

Dear God, We read Thomas Edison made light but in Sunday School they said you did it. I bet he stoled your idea. Sincerely, Donna

Dear God, If you let the dinosaurs not be extinct we would not have a country. You did the right thing. – Jonathan

It seems that, regardless of our age, we have a great deal of difficulty getting a real grasp on the nature of God. If we were to ask a hundred different people about their view of God, we would probably get a hundred different perspectives. These perspectives would be "all over the map."

Some would express an opinion that God is some sort of grandfatherly type who delights in spoiling His children (and even those who are not His children). He only exists, according to some views on this end of the spectrum, to hand out "goodies." He would never think of any form of discipline. God, to some, is not One to pose any kind of threat, nor is He to be taken seriously about much of anything.

On the other hand, others live in a constant fear of God. He exists, at least in their minds, to put them under His microscope. Every deed, word, and thought is scrutinized in order to find sufficient evidence for Him to do what He really wants to do anyway; send them into eternity totally separated from Him. This view of God has Him enjoying nothing more than the spectacle of miserable humans in anguish forever.

Part of the reason that it is so difficult to fully grasp the nature of God is that, like us, He is not one dimensional. Romans 11:22 reminds us of "...the goodness and the severity of God..." The context of that verse is an overview of how God dealt kindly with His people who honored and obeyed Him during the Old Testament dispensation. It contrasts that treatment with His more harsh treatment of those who were disobedient.

Consider the following views of Jesus. In Matt. 12:20, the prophet Isaiah is referred to and this is said about our Lord: "A bruised reed

He will not break, and a smoking flax He will not quench..." A modern equivalent of this might be "Jesus will not kick you while you are down." He is seen here as One who is tender, caring, considerate, etc. After all, is He not the Good Shepherd who deals kindly and tenderly with His sheep? (cf. John 10:1-31)

However, Jesus is not always depicted in ways which are that pleasant to consider. The description found in 2 Thes. 1:7-9 is not nearly as comforting (at least to those who are not obedient to the Lord):

> and to give you who are troubled rest with us when the Lord Jesus is revealed from heaven with His mighty angels, in flaming fire taking vengeance on those who do not know God, and on those who do not obey the gospel of our Lord Jesus Christ. These shall be punished with everlasting destruction from the presence of the Lord and from the glory of His power.

Volumes have been written, sermons have been preached, classes have been taught and still we find it impossible to understand God (cf. Is. 55:8-9). About all we can say with certainty, at least as it relates to this study, is that we need a balanced view of Him.

The reason that is so important is that we need to strive for balance in parenting. In an earlier chapter, we discussed the idea that the proper parenting "method" involved balance. We hope to expand on that here and suggest some helpful things along the way.

We will, once again, use some important principles found in the sixth chapter of Deuteronomy. It has been suggested earlier that this chapter and some of the implications we can make from some of the material in this chapter comprise the best parenting manual we could ever hope for.

There is, in this chapter of God's Word, a wonderful balance that is presented for our consideration. The "shorthand" view of this is that, if parents are to model their parenting style after the model found in this chapter, they will find themselves trying in some ways to emulate God. They will be *firmly loving* and *lovingly firm*.

Please read and consider verses thirteen through nineteen of Deuteronomy six:

> You shall fear the Lord your God and serve Him, and shall take oaths in His name. You shall not go after other gods, the gods of the peoples who are all around you (for the Lord your God is a jealous God among you), lest the anger of the Lord your God be aroused against you and destroy you from the face of the earth.
>
> You shall not tempt the Lord your God as you tempted Him in Massah. You shall diligently keep the commandments of the Lord your God, His testimonies, and His statutes which He has commanded you. And you shall do what is right and good in the sight of the Lord, that it may be well with you, and that you may go in and possess the good land of which the Lord swore to your fathers, to cast out all your enemies from before you, as the Lord has spoken.

It appears to this reader that at least a part of God's message to His people here is "I know what you need; I want you to have it; I have the power to provide it; but I demand respect and obedience." Parents could learn a lot from that!

For some reason, many parents of our day and time are not content with the number of friends their children have. They apparently believe they need two more – Dad and Mom.

Our children do not need two more friends. They desperately need **parents**!

A number of years ago, Paul Harvey wrote the following. It would be my desire that every father would have the same sentiments he had when he wrote these words.

I Am Going to Stay a Father

At a time when being a buddy to one's son is popular, I am going to stay a father. I believe it may yet prove to have been a bit of sad psychology when dads are called 'Jim, Peter, Art, Tom or Jack' by their children. When Spock, Freud, Dewey, and William James have conspired to make dad a minor stockholder on the home's board of directors, when women's rights, civil rights, people's rights, children's rights, and property rights have made it wrong for fathers to speak with authority, I am going to stay a father.

If a gap exists between my sons and daughters and myself, I am going to work hard to understand. But I am also going work hard to be understood…

When they tell it like it is, I will listen, even if I like it better like it was. If old-fashioned things as prayer, Bible study, worship and faith in God ever seem to my children to be out of it, square or whatever – I trust God's help to have faith enough to yet pray for them, and I pledge with Job, to offer up additional sacrifices for them.

With love in our home I will answer their questions about the facts of life, at nudeness and lewdness I refuse to wink. Drinking and smoking are as out of place and unwanted in my home as profanity or the plague. And if experimentation with drugs or marijuana is ever a problem, it will be in violation of my every prayer and request. No laissez faire attitude will be accepted here – even if the weed is legalized and social "tripping" becomes as acceptable as social drinking.

I want my children to know that I make mistakes, that I am foolish, proud and often inconsistent. But I will not tolerate that as an excuse for my hypocrisy. I ask them to help me change as children should, and to expect me to help them change in the methods expected of a parent. Others may look to the under 30 crowd for the wisdom to throw away the past and to say what will remain for future generations; others may let the off-spring in the house determine the foods, the music, and the spending of the household, but I am going to stay a father.

It is my very firm conviction that one of the major reasons that our society and the church are both experiencing some of the challenges we are presently dealing with is that *too many have been (and are being) reared in homes where respect was neither earned nor demanded by the parents.* How many children grow up in homes where they experience something like the following: Something displeases the parent and he or she says, "If you don't stop, I'm going to spank you." Nothing changes and a few minute later, the message is, "Didn't you hear me. I'm really going to spank you!" Still later, "You'd better stop!" Even later, "I'm going to count to three!!!" Maybe that's followed by, "I'm only going to tell you one more time!!!!"

If that is the environment in which a child is reared what view of God are they going to have? When they make the connection that God is our Father, will they not see Him as One who may threaten, but who is never to really be taken seriously?

Wouldn't it be tragic if a child lost his or her soul due in part to the fact that he or she was reared by parents without sufficient backbone to earn and demand respect? A parent who does not earn and demand respect demonstrates a lack of genuine concern for the child. That child will never fully reach his/her potential without the proper training in this area. This type of child will have difficulty with authority throughout his or her entire lifetime.

Furthermore, a parent who is lax in this area demonstrates a lack of concern for himself or herself. How self-respecting is it to let others (even your children) constantly use you as a doormat, an object of ridicule, etc.?

This type of parent also demonstrates a lack of concern for God. After all, He is the One who provided the best parenting instructions available. If we ignore them, what does that say about our estimation of, and dedication to, Him?

It seems as though Erma Bombeck and Paul Harvey were on the same page regarding parenting. It might not hurt for us to consider some of Mrs. Bombeck's thoughts she wrote at one time:

Someday I'll Tell My Children

"You don't love me!" How many times have your children laid that on you? And how many times have you as a parent resisted the urge to tell them how much?

Someday, when my children are old enough to understand the logic that motivates a mother, I'll tell them:

I loved you enough to bug you about where you were going, with whom and what time you would get home.

I loved you enough to be silent and let you discover that your hand-picked friend was a creep.

I loved you enough to make you return a Milky Way with a bite out of it to a drugstore and confess, 'I stole this.'

I loved you enough to stand over you for two hours while you cleaned your bedroom; a job that would have taken me 15 minutes.

I loved you enough to not make excuses for your bad manners.

I loved you enough to ignore 'what every other mother' did.

I loved you enough to let you stumble, fall, and fail so that you could learn to stand alone.

I loved you enough to accept you for what you are, not for what I wanted you to be.

But most of all, I loved you enough to say 'no' when you hated me for it. That was the hardest part of all.

We have discussed the subject of discipline. We do not intend here to spend an inappropriate amount of time on that subject. We would merely suggest, once more, that discipline involves such things as training, example, education, communication, and (yes, when needed) punishment.

Deuteronomy six is not all about discipline and formal training. We suggested in an earlier chapter that "informal training" or "teachable moments" were a part of what is under discussion in this chapter.

The material found in verses 21ff. suggests that what some call "storytelling" can play a vital role in the family experience. *Contrary to what some people believe, all history did not begin with them.* This is true, of course, as far as world affairs goes. It is also true in families.

The Jews who followed God's directives found in this material handed down to their children a wonderful legacy. They knew of their history, their special relationship with God, and a host of others things.

Children today would benefit from knowing something about their "roots." Most families have a "weird uncle" or two. As unbelievable as this may seem, those family stories told about those uncles and other relatives are important in a child (and later an adult) feeling a sense of belonging and/or connectedness.

I know that the older I get the more I cherish those long ago memories of the "storytelling" my parents and other relatives did. My wife can easily recall lying on her bed as a child and listening to some of her aunts and uncles, as well as her parents and grandparents, "swapping stories" on her grandmother's front porch next door. This was in the days before her parents had air conditioning. That meant that her bedroom window was open. That gave her "a front row seat."

The stories I heard as a child, the stories my wife heard as a child, and the stories that children would benefit from today might be repetitive. The children might hear the same story so often that they begin to feel as though they could tell it better than their relatives. Instead of being an argument *against* storytelling, this may, in fact, be an argument *for* this practice.

A study of the Passover observance is an example of this. It will be remembered that the people being spoken to in Deuteronomy six are the "younger generation" of the people who were originally given the plan for the Passover. Almost all of those who were above the age of twenty when the instructions were first given had perished in the wilderness.

The pattern for observing the Passover would help to ensure uniformity in its observance regardless of what generation or what time it would be observed. If one would take the time to read God's original instructions as given in Exodus 13:3-16, it will become clear that storytelling is a "built in" part of this observance. Succeeding generations turned this into an elaborate and formal ritual, but it still was "the same old story" that was repeated year after year.

I am convinced that children need to know about the "spiritual exodus" of their parents and other family members. It would help them to know how their parents and other relatives became Christians; who influenced them; some of the events that were instrumental in that decision-making process; and a host of other factors. This information might do more good than we could imagine in helping young people as they develop their own faith.

I believe that "storytelling" about what has come to be known as the Restoration Movement might also be helpful; at least to some degree. I am not sure what I did or did not know about such men as Alexander Campbell, Thomas Campbell, "Racoon" John Smith, Barton W. Stone, etc. when I was baptized. I do, however, remember my father speaking despairingly about the "Campbellites."

I was convinced by a young lady who became my wife and by some of the preaching I heard where she worshiped that I needed to do what people did in the first century. I was compelled by the logic that I would be a member of the same church of which they were members if I did what they did.

I am convinced that I would never have entertained thoughts like that on my own had it not been for the influence of people who had followed the example of the "pioneers of the Restoration Movement" by relying solely on God's Word for their authority in matters of religion. I did not then, nor do I now, have any interest in following the teachings of the Campbells and others, merely because they were men of great intellect and insight.

I do, however, have a great deal of interest in following their example in a search for truth. Parents need to set the example in this as well as in so many other things. Children need to know that Dad and Mom have a resolve to search for, understand, and obey the truth as contained in God's holy Word.

In a day and time when there are those who are willing to disregard basic biblical truths, including the mode and purpose of baptism, *I believe that my generation needs to "hand off" a tenacious dedication to the bedrock principles upon which the members of any generation can build their lives.* Each generation needs to be concerned with, and involved in, restoration. A basic understanding of what this means and how others have tried to achieve this is important.

If Deuteronomy six teaches anything, it teaches the absolute necessity of a keen awareness of God. God is presented as the One whom we are to love with all of our being. It is His Word that is to be studied, treasured, and passed on to succeeding generations. He is presented as the One who works in the affairs of men and women. Ultimately, it is God who will punish and who will reward.

It is hoped that every parent will take seriously his/her responsibility to pass on the greatest legacy that can be passed on. While it is true that God has no grandchildren, parents can do much in helping their children see how important God is to them. They can help their children understand how they believe that God has been at work in their lives. They can help children see about dedication and service, rather than merely reading about it or hearing about it.

There is a most interesting and challenging word picture presented in Psalm 127:3-4:

> Behold, children are a heritage from the Lord, the fruit of the womb is a reward. Like arrows in the hand of a warrior, So are the children of one's youth.

Most of us would agree with and to some extent understand the thought that our children are a special gift from God, but what is the message about children being arrows? What implications can be drawn from this word picture?

It occurs to me that a warrior does not shoot arrows aimlessly. He chooses a target, takes much care in taking aim, and then (maybe somewhat reluctantly) releases the arrow. Does that sound familiar?

Shouldn't Christian parents be doing all they can while they can to "aim" their children at heaven? Why then do so many parents seem to have no such goal in mind for their children? They seem to be so busy aiming their children at goals that have only a worldly application and take little or no time to point them in the direction of heaven.

On March 14, 1998, I walked down an aisle of a church building in Tennessee and gave my daughter's hand to a young man who had won her heart. I then took the Bible (which contained the wedding ceremony) from the hand of his grandfather who is also a preacher and I struggled to perform their wedding ceremony. When

I introduced for the first time Mr. and Mrs. Jeremiah Tatum, I felt an arrow leave my hand.

On June 5, 1999, I was honored to serve as my son's best man as he gave his name to a young lady who already had his heart. As I heard her brother (another preacher) say that they were husband and wife and introduce Mr. and Mrs. Adam Faughn, I felt the second and last arrow leave my hand.

Looking back on the experience of rearing our two children, it seems that we only had them for such a short time. I can only pray now that I aimed them correctly and that they are on their way to the eternal promised land.

I wish that, before they were born or when they were very small, somebody had helped me to understand some principles from Deuteronomy six. It might have helped to reinforce what their mother and I were already trying to do.

It is my very fervent prayer that what has been presented here will be helpful to others who are blessed with the challenge to "...bring (children) up in the training and admonition of the Lord." (Eph. 6:4)

What Part do the Children Play?

10

What Part do the Children Play?

Think about much of the material you've heard or read about families. Don't most of the lessons follow one or more of the following tracks?

One of the familiar tracks is for speakers, teachers, writers and others to try to impress upon our young people the need to be the right kind of person by using some great Bible characters as examples. How many lessons have you hear on the theme "Dare to be a Daniel"? How many times have you or your children heard about the good qualities that people like Joseph, Samuel, David, and Timothy had when they were young?

On the other hand, how many have traveled on another track to try to teach some needed truths? How many times have we been warned by the behavior of other Bible characters? Hophni and Phinehas, the sons of Eli, come to mind, as do such characters as the young people who mocked Elisha, some of David's children, and others.

If the tactic being used does not involve character studies, maybe a familiar text is employed. Maybe young people are reminded to "Remember now your Creator in the days of your youth, before the difficult days come, and the years draw near when you say, 'I have no pleasure in them'" (Eccl. 12:1).

The text could just as easily be Eph. 6:1-3:

Children, obey your parents in the Lord, for this is right. 'Honor your father and mother,' which is the first commandment with promise: 'that it may be well with you and you may live long on the earth.'

Regardless of what approach is taken, all too often the message received has more to do with the role of parents in the family and/ or the role of the children in society. Very little of a practical nature is presented concerning the role of children in the family unit.

The children may hear that they are "the church of tomorrow" and hear how they are to be productive members of society *someday*, but they may never get the idea that they have roles to play in the family in which they are being reared. If this is the case, it is little wonder that some young people just "hang out" and/or "do their own thing" until they reach physical maturity only to discover that they have a long, long way to go before reaching emotional, social, and spiritual maturity.

The information in this chapter will not answer every question, nor will it be a roadmap that will lead every child to his or her desired destiny and the family to true harmony. The information presented in this chapter is taken from the very familiar account of the events recorded in the latter part of Luke 2. We have used this passage in an earlier chapter. We will return again to the events involving Jesus being left in Jerusalem by Joseph and Mary.

One of the more interesting choices of words is Luke's reference to Joseph and Mary as "His **parents**..." (Luke 2:41, emphasis added). As we all know, Joseph was Mary's husband, but God was Jesus' Father. This choice of words makes the material in the remainder of this chapter applicable to every child and every family. There are many situations in our world and society today that have resulted in a child being reared by one or more parents who are not his or her biological parents. The child may be being reared by two people who loved him/her enough to provide a home through the process of adoption. Death, desertion, or divorce may have produced a situation whereby a child is being reared by one biological parent, but not by both.

The situations are varied and each one is unique, but the people who choose to raise a child who may not be "theirs" biologically deserve no less respect than those who are rearing their biological children. At the same time the children in such an arrangement should be treated no differently than biological children should be treated.

In most of these cases, the children are part of the family because of a definite decision. In the case of an adoption, the parents made a very definite decision to rear the child as their own. In the case of step-children, they were also part of the decision-making process (or at least they should have been). When one chooses to marry a partner who has a child or children, he or she needs to be able to accept them as well as the new spouse and to provide the same nurturing atmosphere in which to mature as they would, or do, for their own children.

There does not need to be any thought on the part of the stepparent that "You're not really mine, so I don't have to treat you like I do my own children." At the same time, one of the challenges for any child in this situation is to refrain from thinking or saying, "Your're not my Dad/Mom. You can't tell me what to do." It is more than just a little significant that, after the events in Jerusalem, we read the following about Jesus, "Then He went down and came to Nazareth, and was subject to **them**..." (Luke 2:51, emphasis added).

What exactly can be learned from the text to which reference has already been made? What are some of the things young people need to consider as they read this familiar account?

For one thing, when Joseph and Mary returned to Jerusalem, they found Jesus doing something honorable. According to Luke's record of these events, "Now so it was that after three days they found Him in the temple, sitting in the midst of the teachers, both listening to them and asking them questions" (Luke 2:46). I find it interesting that this twelve year old young man who was left to His own devices was doing something that would, in no way, embarrass His parents.

I'm wondering if that could be said about all young people. I'm wondering if some would not succumb to the temptation to do something *very* dishonorable if they knew their parents were nowhere around. Maybe the question needs to be asked, "What will I do (or what **do** I do) when I am in a situation when I'm 'all on my own' at age 12, or at age 16, or at age 21?" Do I (or will I) do anything that would embarrass my parents when I'm just hanging out with my friends; when I'm away from them at school; when my boyfriend/girlfriend and I are all alone; when I'm away at college; or in any other similar situation.

As I write these words, I am on "the wrong side" of sixty years of age. My parents have both been gone from this life for a number of years. I do not share the convictions they had religiously, but I do know that they were very moral people. At what I know young people would see as a *very* advanced age, I am still aware of what impact my behavior has on their training and their memory. Young people would do well to consider this as well.

They would also do well to consider the following passages from Proverbs:

- "Even a child is known by his deeds, whether what he does is pure and right" (20:11).
- "The father of the righteous will greatly rejoice, and he who begets a wise child will delight in him. Let your father and your mother be glad, and let her who bore you rejoice" (23:24-25).

It would be good if young people would consider how their parents say the following sentence: "That's my son/daughter." Is it said with pride because of the kind of person the young person has shown himself/herself to be? Is it said with a kind of resignation or remorse?

As we have already noticed, Jesus was subject to Joseph and Mary (cf. Luke 2:51). It might be helpful to explore some of the implications of this concept and of the word "subject." The authorities on the Greek language tell us that this word is translated from a Greek word that is actually a combination of two words. The first of these words carries with it the meaning that is placed beneath something else. The second word has to do with an orderly arrangement.

I find this extremely interesting. My interest intensifies when I find other places in the New Testament where this word, or at least one form of this word, is used. The discussion of our relationship with and responsibilities to civil governing authorities in Romans 13:1-7 is one of those places. There are others, but this one should be sufficient to help us to understand that God is concerned about order and that nothing works the way He intended it to work when His prescribed order gets "out of whack."

If anybody had a right to exercise authority over His parents, it was Jesus. When He referred to "...My Father's business" (Luke 2:49), He was most definitely not speaking of carpentry. At age twelve, He knew that God was His Father and could have "pulled rank" on Joseph and Mary, but did not do so. He knew that God's design for the family included the children being in subjection to the parents.

We might also notice an interesting tidbit from the words of Jesus in Matthew 21:28-30. We normally use this passage to demonstrate what repentance is. In this passage a father says to both of his sons, "Son, go work today in my vineyard" (Matt. 21:28, see also v. 30).

It is worth noticing that the father in this passage did not say, "Son, if you don't have anything else to do..."; "Son, whenever you want to..."; "Son, I'd like for you to..."; "Son, you may not want to do this and, if you don't I understand, but..."; etc. Apparently, Jesus thought that fathers have the right to make demands of their children and that the children are expected to meet those demands. "Because I said so" is still a valid reason for a child to be expected to do something a parent tells him or her to do.

While we are on the subject of work and as a short departure from Luke 2, this might be an appropriate place to suggest that young people need to learn the value of work. While the "Father's business" to which Jesus referred in Luke 2:49 was not carpentry, it appears that He did, in fact, learn that trade. In Matt. 13:55, He is referred to as "the carpenter's son," but in Mark 6:3, He is referred to as "the carpenter." Apparently, somewhere along the way Joseph had taught him his trade.

This was in keeping with the Jewish thought that a father who did not teach a child to work taught him to be a thief. Parents today would do well to learn a lesson from that.

However, children need to also learn from this. Far too many grow up thinking that the world always owes them something. Maybe a little "negotiation" early in life would solve some of that. Any child who thinks he or she needs to be paid for every chore done around the house might need to be presented a bill for rent, meals, etc.!

The Bible says a lot about laziness and none of it is good. There is even one verse that addresses the laziness of children: "He who gathers in summer is a wise son; he who sleeps in harvest is a son who causes shame" (Prov. 10:5). As young people grow up in a family environment, they need to learn, "Whatever your hand finds to do, do it with your might; for there is no work or device or knowledge or wisdom in the grave where you are going" (Eccl. 9:10).

It is possible that the most well-known verse in Luke 2 is the last one: "And Jesus increased in wisdom and stature, and in favor with God and men." (v. 52) There is no telling how much material has been presented on this four-fold growth of Jesus and how each person needs to grow intellectually, physically, spiritually, and socially.

Yes, parents, as well as elders, preachers, Bible class teachers and others can help provide an environment conducive to this type of growth. At the same time, young people need to "step up to the plate" and take the initiative to grow in these areas.

It is a concern of mine that many young people are cheating their parents, themselves, and God by failing to take advantage of opportunities for growth in these areas. For example, far too many people find out way too late in life that they should have taken more of an interest in their own education. All of us probably know a number of people who wish they could turn the clock back and have another chance to make more of an effort to learn what their school teachers were trying to teach them. Now, they realize that they do not have the necessary qualifications for a career they want, they've disappointed their parents in this respect, and they failed to use the mental ability given to them by God.

In a somewhat similar way, many young people fail to get a proper amount of physical exercise and consume what is far less than the best diet. Even worse, some precious young people are lured by worldly and evil influences to ingest substances that are both illegal and harmful; to do things with their bodies that are dangerous; and/or to seemingly look for ways to abuse themselves physically. What probably comes to mind initially is the impact this type of lifestyle has on one of the four previously mentioned areas; it affects the person physically.

However, it has an effect on all of the other aspects of our lives as well. It has been demonstrated that our physical condition has an effect on our ability to learn, retain and utilize knowledge. While it may not be the way it *should* be, the fact remains that people who are far from the "norm" physically will suffer socially as well.

In addition to this, a failure to take proper care of our bodies is neglecting to take responsibility for the "...temple of the Holy Spirit..." (1 Cor. 6:19). Interestingly enough, the immediate context of that phrase has to do with sexual activity outside the marriage relationship. It is necessary for Christians of any age to remember Paul's inspired words in 1 Corinthians 6:20: "For you were bought with a price; therefore glorify God in your body and in your spirit, which are God's."

A lot of wonderful things can be said about people. Both during one's life and after one has departed this life, it is nice to hear complimentary things about people. One such inspired compliment is found in James 2:23:

And the Scripture was fulfilled which says, 'Abraham believed God, and it was accounted to him for righteousness.' And he was called the friend of God.

Can you not think of things that would be **much** worse than to be referred to as a *friend of God*? I would not presume to know why the Holy Spirit decided to list spiritual growth immediately after physical growth in the description of our Lord in the years following his experiences in the temple at age twelve. One possibility might be that He was aware of the fact that there are many who are physical giants, but who are spiritual midgets.

Our Lord, of course, could not have been described in that way. His followers today should not be so described either.

As I write these words, I am very keenly aware of some people who are very limited physically. Some of the limitations are due to illness, various physical deformities, accidents, and a host of other factors. Others are due to the aging process. The reasons for physical limitations are almost endless.

However, it has been my observation, that a great many of these people who are limited in this way demonstrate a spirituality that they might not otherwise have had if they were in perfect health. Not only so, but they "preach" very effective sermons to others by how they deal with the adversities that have come their way.

This is not to say that one must make a choice to either increase in stature or to increase in favor with God. It would be my prayer that God would bless every young person with good physical health and a close relationship with Him.

However, the point needs to be made that, if a choice needs to be made, the better choice is to find favor with God. Our young people are growing up in a society (and, in far too many cases, in families) where the emphasis is on entertainment, material possessions, luxury, pleasure, etc.

All too often, God gets "lost in the shuffle" as some of these young people (and older people as well) try to deal with all that we often think of as very important. Paul reminded Timothy "...that from childhood you have known the Holy Scriptures, which are able to make you wise for salvation through faith which is in Christ Jesus" (2 Tim. 3:15).

To be sure, Timothy's mother and grandmother played an important role in his spiritual maturity (cf. 2 Tim. 1:5). At the same time, Timothy, himself, had to assume his part of the responsibility for this maturity.

There needs to be some quality time spent away from the various venues of entertainment, from sports, and even from schoolwork in order to spend time letting God talk to the heart of young people through His Word and allowing for sufficient time for the young people to pour out their hearts to God in prayer. Friends communicate. Young people would be well advised to adopt a lifestyle very early that would enable them to do this.

We are social creatures. At the earliest of times in the history of mankind, it was God who said, "It is not good that man should be alone..." (Gen. 2:18). Somewhere along the way, some of us may have given our young people the idea that there is a choice to make. The choice they may think they have to make is that they can either be a disciple of Jesus or they can have friends, but they cannot do both. According to this way of thinking, Christians are, by definition, isolated from everybody around them and those who get along with others are incapable of following God.

I'm not sure where we got that idea, but it wasn't from the Bible. Even a casual study of the earthly ministry of our Lord demonstrates a type of personality and a lifestyle that attracted, not repelled, people. He was invited to weddings, banquets, and other social events. People seem to have been "drawn" to Him.

In a similar manner, the early church is described as "...praising God and having favor with all the people..." (Acts 2:47). This would not have been the case if these people were totally inept socially.

It is, of course, the clear teaching of the Bible that "...friendship of the world is enmity with God..." (James 4:4). We cannot "sell out" to the world. We cannot compromise truth for friendship or trade spirituality for popularity. At the same time we cannot "...light a lamp and put it under a basket..." (Matt. 5:15). If we are to be the salt and light that our Lord wants us to be, we must come into contact with, and learn how to reach, others. (cf. Matt. 5:13-16).

Learning social skills and graces is not the equivalent of denying the faith. The earlier we learn that, the more well-adjusted and happier we will be. The family setting is a wonderful atmosphere in which to learn this important lesson.

The closing verses of Luke 2, as well as other passages written about the earthly ministry of Christ, can be used to help young people see their role in their family, in God's family, and in society as a whole. It is the prayer of the one writing these words that young people will learn these valuable lessons and insights from our Lord.

What if they don't? What if young people fail to learn lessons about doing honorable things (even when left on their own), respect, authority, work, and the need to grow in the same four areas in which our Lord grew?

The good news (really very bad news) is that there are places custom-tailored for this type of person. The person who never accepts responsibility for his or her own actions and has never learned to respect anybody's authority is more than welcome there. He or she can just lie around and "veg out" if that is the desire. There may be opportunities for growth or change, but, in reality, none is really expected. Along with all of this, a bed, clothing, and meals are all provided! They may not be the type of bed that would be preferred; the wardrobe may be limited; and there is not much choice on the menu, but all of this *is provided at the local jail and/or at penitentiaries across our nation*!!

Part of the reason for writing this chapter has been due to my desire to do what I can to keep young people out of those places. My desire is for them to live a life of faithful, dedicated, fulfilling service to the One who gave His life for them and to enjoy His fellowship throughout all eternity.

Paul wrote to Timothy about those who, among other things, were "...disobedient to parents..." (2 Timothy 3:2). He told him to turn away from these people (v. 5).

In some very serious and sobering language used in Romans 1, Paul writes of "...the wrath of God..." (v. 1) and about some people about whom it is said that "...God gave them up..." (vs. 24, 26). These people were guilty of a lot of things, not the least of which was being "...disobedient to parents" (v. 30).

Young people have responsibilities in families that have an impact on the family, on their future, and on their eternal destiny. It **is** important after all to "Remember now your Creator in the days of your youth..." (Eccl. 12:1).

The Sandwich Generation

The Sandwich Generation

Ah, the good old days. How often do we look through rose-colored glasses and long for the life that the fictional Walton family had on the long running television series.

The pace of life was slower; there was more of a sense of belonging in both families and communities; and at least one set of grandparents was always around to lend advice. Wouldn't it have been great to have lived then?

Those who did live during the time in which *The Waltons* was set may have a somewhat different perspective. I did a little research into the 1930's and, indeed, it would be nice to pay 14 cents for a quart of milk, 9 cents for a loaf of bread, and 40 cents for a pound of round steak.

However, most of us would not prefer the average annual income of that decade of $1,368.00. It might, though, be preferable to **no** work. The unemployment rate during that time was 25%.

There is another major difference between those "good old days" of the Waltons and our era. This difference may be as big a challenge as many of the others. This is particularly true when it comes to family relationships, responsibilities, and opportunities.

There is a good chance that a family portrait of the Walton family would not include grandpa and grandma. The life expectancy at that time was 58.1 years for men and 61 years for women.

It comes as no news that our life expectancy continues to inch upward. As I write this, the average for people of both sexes is 78.8 years.

I have also found in various sources the following information which I thought was interesting.

- There are approximately 35 million people (about 13% of the population) living in the U.S. today who are sixty-five years of age or older. I found this particularly interesting when I learned that the entire population of Canada is about 32.5 million.
- 2/3 of the people who have ever lived to age sixty-five are alive today.
- There are 50,000 people in our nation who have lived at least a century.
- Six to eight million elderly people in our nation need help with basic needs such as getting out of bed and taking care of personal hygiene.
- Millions more of the elderly need help with such things as meals, handling their money, and transportation.
- What I found of particular interest are the following two reported facts:
- More than half of frail older people who are unmarried (most have lost a spouse) obtain help from daughter, including nearly 2/3 of those receiving help with basic personal needs.
- More than half of adult children helping their frail older parents are employed.

Can you say, "juggling?" Look at the picture painted by these facts. In millions of families in our society, there are people who are trying to juggle responsibilities to their spouse, their employer, their friends, etc. while at the same time feeling a need to help elderly parents with some very basic (and often not too pleasant) tasks. A great many of these same people have children at home and/or may have married children and grandchildren with whom they would like to spend some time, energy, and resources.

It is little wonder that, years ago, somebody coined the term "Sandwich Generation" to refer to these people. They do see themselves "in the middle." They see themselves as the "ingredient" that holds the whole thing together. Somewhere I read that the average woman in our nation spends about as much time helping elderly parents as she does in rearing children.

What does the future hold? According to some material I've read by the year 2020 there will be 70 million people over the age of sixty-five and 18 million over the age of eighty-five. By the year 2030 it is projected that *for the first time in our history* the percentage of our population under the age of seventeen will be *smaller than* the percentage over the age of 65.

Does the Bible address this issue at all? Does it give "the sandwich generation" any insight as to their responsibilities toward their aging parents? I believe that it does.

First of all, the Bible is honest (as it is in all things) about some of the challenges the aging process presents. For example, Psalm 31:10-13 depicts the loneliness felt by (and, sadly, experienced by) those who are older. How sad it is when those who are older are "put on a shelf" by others; especially by those who should love them the most.

The physical limitations that the aging process brings on are discussed in God's Word as well. Probably the most well known passage along this line is Ecclesiastes 12:1-8. A very graphic (and sometimes all too real) depiction of some of the effects of old age are to be found in this passage.

Along with this passage, we might also want to consider 1 Kings 1 wherein David is depicted in his latter days as being unable to keep warm. I'm sure some "sandwich generation" folks have been almost run out the room of their parents because the thermostat was set so high it seemed that water could boil without being on a stove.

We might also readily identify with the poor eyesight that an elderly Isaac had. In his case, it caused him not to be able to distinguish between his two sons. It may never get to that point with us and/or our relatives, but most of us get used to glasses, contacts, corrective surgery, or some sort of help for our diminishing eyesight as we age.

There is an interesting passage to be found in Zechariah 8:4-5. We will let others debate about the exact meaning of this prophecy and its fulfillment. Our purpose here is to focus on something else. The passage states:

> Thus says the Lord of hosts: 'Old men and old women shall again sit in the streets of Jerusalem, each one with his staff in his hand because of great age. The streets of the city shall be full of boys and girls playing in its streets.'

Isn't it interesting that the prophet sees the presence of elderly people who need to use a cane as a blessing *along with* the enthusiasm and energy of the youth? Apparently, aging is not to be viewed entirely in a negative light either by those of us who are rapidly approaching the need for the use of a cane or by those of us who have somebody like this in our family.

Repeatedly the Bible teaches that the elderly are deserving of respect. In Leviticus 19:31 we read, "You shall rise before the gray headed and honor the presence of an old man, and fear your God: I am the Lord." An interesting caveat is found in Proverbs 16:31: "The silver-haired head is a crown of glory, if it is found in the way of righteousness."

It seems to me that there is a two-pronged lesson in those two passages. Children need to learn to respect the elderly. Our society needs to be reminded of that. Also, we need to live our lives so that we deserve respect in our "golden years." There are some who need to learn that lesson as well.

"Honor your father and your mother." These words are found repeatedly in God's Word. They comprise one of the Ten Commandments (Ex. 20:12), but we find that same sentiment repeated by our Lord and by the apostle Paul (cf. Matt. 19:19; Eph. 6:2). I conclude, then, that God has always intended for children to honor their parents.

As I read the Scriptures, I also conclude that this honor is to be demonstrated by *adult* parents to aging parents. One of the great confrontations that our Lord had with some of His day had to do with a "loophole" they had devised to keep them from taking care of their parents. Jesus was not talking to children in Mark 7:1-13; He was talking to adults.

It might also need to be pointed out that we sometimes make a somewhat incorrect application of 1 Timothy 5:8. The verse reads, "But if anyone does not provide for his own, and especially for those of his household, he has denied the faith and is worse than an unbeliever." The application many make of this passage is that we are to provide for our spouses and our children. While this is true, the context of the passage shows that the primary meaning has to do with taking care of the older widows in a family.

There are examples in the Bible of those who demonstrated respect, care, and concern for their parents. In Genesis 47:11-12, we find the information telling us about how Joseph made sure his aging father, as well as his brothers and their families, were able to dwell in the best part of Egypt. Matthew 8:14-15 informs us that Peter's mother-in-law was living in the home of Peter and his family. Of course, the ultimate example of taking care of a parent is Jesus. On the cross, Jesus made sure that His mother would be taken care of (cf. John 19:26-27).

For a negative example of all of this, one has only to read Proverbs 30:11-14. Sadly, many of our day and time can be described by the following words:

There is a generation that curses its father, and does not bless its mother. There is a generation that is pure in its own eyes, yet is not washed from its filthiness. There is a generation--oh, how lofty are their eyes! And their eyelids are lifted up. There is a generation whose teeth are like swords, and whose fangs are like knives, to devour the poor from off the earth, and the needy from among men.

How does one try to sum up in one chapter in a book what could be useful as people attempt to deal with the challenges presented by the aging process, especially as it relates to those whom we love? What scriptural and practical advice can be given and how can it be condensed into something that would be easy for one to remember in any situation at any time?

The best answer I can come up with to those questions can be found in Matthew 7:12: "Therefore, whatever you want men to do to you, do also to them, for this is the Law and the Prophets." Over the years, this has come to be known as "The Golden Rule."

Accordingly, the remainder of this chapter will be devoted to what I am calling –

THE GOLDEN RULE FOR THE GOLDEN YEARS

There are some implications of this "rule" I would like for us to explore; especially as they relate to the elderly. The first of these is ---

WE ALL KNOW HOW WE WOULD LIKE TO BE TREATED

You've probably heard the old joke about the Boy Scout that showed up at the scout meeting with bruises and with his uniform all torn and tattered and dirty. When he was asked what happened, he reported that it was all a result of him trying to do his good deed for the day. When he was asked what that deed was, he said, "I was trying to help a little old lady across the street." When it was suggested to him that it seemed strange that he got in the shape he was in while trying to do that, he said, "But the thing is; she didn't want to go across the street!"

There is more than a kernel of truth to that story. We may be trying to assist somebody who is older without realizing what they really want or need. You would **not** be doing me a big favor if you brought me a "mess of greens" to eat. I know what I like to eat – *and it is not greens*!

We need to remember that this situation does not change as a person gets older. Each older person knows what he or she wants. We will discuss the individual aspect of all of this later, but, for now, let us look at some general observations.

I grew up thinking Art Linkletter was just a man who said funny things on television and/or who got others (especially children) to say funny things. I've found out that there was a very serious side to this man.

Years ago, I read a book by him entitled *Old Age is Not for Sissies* (New York: Viking Penguin, Inc., 1988). The material below is from page thirty-eight of that book:

Golden Rights of Senior Americans

1. Irrespective of individual status or achievement, Senior Americans have the right to expect to be held in high esteem and treated with consideration and dignity because of age alone.
2. Senior Americans have the right to independence, privacy and choice of persons with whom they live and associate; they also have the right not to fear abridgement of those rights because of advancing age.
3. In all instances where decisions governing personal health are concerned, Senior Americans have the right to complete and accurate information necessary to ensure freedom of choice in selection of health care services. They have the further right to expect medical treatment from persons whose knowledge is strengthened with compassion and whose judgment is governed by moral restraint.
4. Senior Americans have the right to manage their financial affairs, as well as the right to complete information and full disclosure of possible consequences from those through whom they seek assistance with the management of those affairs.
5. Senior Americans have the right to freedom from fear of mental and physical abuse, as well as from chemical or physical restraint except in medical emergencies.

6. Senior Americans have the right to the information and assistance needed to ensure a continuing healthy lifestyle.
7. Senior Americans have the right to choose how and with whom they spend leisure time, as well as the right to expect considerate assistance when they travel.

Maybe your list would be longer; maybe it would be shorter; maybe there would be some changes. The point is that senior citizens know what they want. It seems to me that the next logical implication, then, would be ---

COMMUNICATION

Isn't it sad that we feel like we need to read books, go to hear an "expert," or find some other source of information about the needs of elderly parents – especially *our* elderly parents? One author has written, "I have seldom been in an unstructured conversation about old age with anybody, young or old, that lasted more than five minutes." (Tim Stafford, "The Old Age Heresy, *Christianity Today*, 9/16/91, p. 30)

Maybe, as sort of a starting point, the following material might be helpful. It can be found on pages 13-14 of *Your Aging Parents; When and How to Help* by Margaret Anderson. According to a study cited by Ms. Anderson, the desires of the elderly are ---

- Security; having enough funds to live a comfortable, independent life
- Association with other people – Communication and a sense of belonging
- Recognition of knowledge and skills – Mental stimulation – New opportunities for learning
- Autonomy – the right to live alone and make their own decisions as long as they are able

The author also makes this pertinent point: "Christians who are elderly speak of a hope that their children will remain true to their faith."

To be sure, there are barriers to good communication and the aging process may present some of its own. Not the least of these challenges is the one presented when hearing begins to deteriorate. We may get to the point of the elderly couple I heard about who had celebrated their sixtieth wedding anniversary. After all of the rest of the family was gone, the husband looked at his wife and said, "I'm proud of you." The wife replied, "I'm tired of you, too."

It *is* frustrating to repeat most of what is said, but much can be gained if we learn to communicate with those who are older. "Wisdom is with aged men, and with length of days, understanding" (Job 12:12).

It was Mark Twain who made this observation: When I was a boy of 14, my father was so ignorant I could hardly stand to have the old man around. But when I got to be 21, I was astonished at how much the old man had learned in seven years."

ACTION

James reminds us that faith is demonstrated in action (cf. James 2:14-26). Similarly, *love* is demonstrated in *doing* something for our parents, not in just saying, "I love you."

On pages 376-377 of *The Family Matters Handbook*, the following suggestions are made under the heading of "Giving the Blessing to Your Parents":

1. "Your parents need you to *meaningfully touch* them."
2. "They also need *spoken words* from their children."
3. "When you bless your parents with words that *attach high value* to them, you can be a tremendous encouragement in their lives."
4. "Parents need words that picture a *special future* for them." (The author mentions the importance of heaven, but also includes

such things as asking them for advice and letting them be a part of your future – your children.

5. "Of all the ways you can bless your parents, the genuine commitment to walk with your parents through each step in life is particularly important at the end of their lives."

Each situation is different, but the challenge is the same. We need to find something to *do* and not be like the people of Jesus' day whom he criticized because, as He said, they "...say and do not" (Matt. 23:3).

INDIVIDUALITY

Each situation **is** different. We need to recognize that in more ways than one. The wording of "The Golden Rule" makes it personal. The application is universal, but the particulars are not "one size fits all."

First, each older person is different. Those who are trying to assist them need to be aware of each person's needs, desires, etc. We do not need to get ourselves in the shape of the Boy Scout mentioned earlier.

Each person, including those who are older, is important to God. If Luke 12:6-7 teaches anything, it teaches that God does not forget us *as individuals* and that *each of us* is of great value to Him.

However, there is another component to this concept of individuality. Each family has the right to handle things as *they* see fit. Far too much tongue wagging takes place concerning how families decide to take care of these situations. Some are criticized for admitting a loved one into a nursing home while others are criticized for not doing so.

I would suggest that the old Indian admonition to walk a mile in another person's moccasins before offering criticism might be appropriate here. If ever the following admonition from scripture applies with regard to our interpersonal relationships, I believe it applies here: **"Judge not, that you be not judged"** (Matt. 7:1).

SOWING AND REAPING

All who read these words are probably familiar with at least the concept of sowing and reaping. In our day and time, it may be more popular to express this concept as "what goes around comes around," but the more biblical way to express this is:

> Do not be deceived, God is not mocked; for whatever a man sows, that he will also reap. For he who sows to his flesh will of the flesh reap corruption, but he who sows to the Spirit will of the Spirit reap everlasting life (Gal. 6:7-8).

It may be helpful to put those two verses back into their immediate context. We might get a somewhat different perspective than what some may presently have.

It seems that some have the idea that "sowing to the Spirit" involves what might be called "churchy things." There is absolutely nothing wrong with trying to encourage people to study God's Word, have an active and healthy prayer life, assemble with the saints on a regular basis, and other such things. You will not find this author taking the position that none of these things are important as we seek to develop a close relationship with God.

At the same time, the immediate context of the passage above includes working to restore an erring brother (v. 1); bearing each other's burdens (v. 2); not growing weary in well doing (v. 9); and doing good to all as we have opportunity (v. 10). It is beginning to sound like "sowing to the Spirit" may involve me rolling up my sleeves, getting my hands dirty, and helping somebody.

How does this apply to our present discussion? My wife and I tried to see to the needs of one or more of our parents for about twenty years. All of them are now in eternity. More than once, we had two of our parents in the hospital at the same time. At one time, three of our four parents were in the hospital.

At various times, all four parents were either in a nursing home or an assisted living home – or both. At one time, we had one of our parents living in our home. At other times, we had to travel over an hour in order to take care of things we thought needed to be taken care of.

During much of this time, our children were still at home. **We were the sandwich generation.**

Our children had the opportunity to observe how their parents dealt with their own parents. I'm sure that they filed things away, even if only subconsciously.

Now that our children have their own children and are making their own lives, I often wonder how their mother and I will be taken care of if, and when, we become frail and need to be cared for.

How will they react when they are the "sandwich generation?" If I am treated like I treated my parents, will that be a good thing?

Hopefully, this chapter has those who read it to stop and think. I know that, as I wrote it, I did a lot of thinking, reflecting, and praying.

It is hoped that all of us, regardless of age or family situation, will find comfort in these words:

'Blessed are the dead who die in the Lord from now on.' 'Yes,' says the Spirit, 'that they may rest from their labors, and their works follow them' (Rev. 14:13).

Christ in the Home

12

Christc in the Home

I read about a news reporter who went to a location where a house was steadily burning to the ground. A little boy was watching the destruction with his parents. The reporter assumed (correctly) that the structure belonged to them. The reporter said the young boy, "Son, it looks like you don't have a home anymore." The response of the little boy is, to my mind, classic: *"We have a home. We just don't have a house to put it in."*

It seems to me that we have become sort of lazy in our language. By that I mean that we, sometimes, use words interchangeably which, in reality, have slightly different meanings.

For example, not every female who has attained a certain level of physical maturity is a lady. She may be a woman, but she may not be a lady. "Woman" and "lady" are not synonyms, at least as I understand and try to use these words.

As the little boy in the story above correctly helps us to understand, the words "house" and "home" are also not to be used interchangeably. Our street address may be where our house is located, but, as the old adage reminds us, "Home is where the heart is."

In *Illustrations Unlimited*, James S. Hewitt has written these words:

A house is a house is a house – until love comes through the door, that is. And love intuitively goes around sprinkling that special brand of angel dust that transforms a house into a very special home for very special people: your family.

Money, of course, can build a charming house, but only love can furnish it with a feeling of home.

Duty can pack an adequate sack lunch, but love may decide to tuck a little love note inside.

Money can provide a television set, but love controls it and cares enough to say no and take the guff that comes with it.

Obligation sends the children to bed on time, but love tucks the covers in around their necks and passes out kisses and hugs (even to teenagers!).

Obligation can cook a meal, but love embellishes the table with a potted ivy trailing around slender candles.

Duty writes many letters, but love tucks a joke or a picture or fresh gum inside.

Compulsion keeps a sparkling house, but love and prayer stand a better chance of producing a happy family.

Duty gets offended quickly if it isn't appreciated, but love learns to laugh a lot and work for the sheer joy of doing it.

Obligation can pour a glass of milk, but love will add a little chocolate. (Wheaton: Tyndale House Publishers, Inc., 1988; p. 192)

In the remainder of this chapter, we will take a short look at four homes visited by our Savior while He was on the earth. It is hoped that we will learn something from this short study that will help us to see what blessings are available to us as we invite Jesus into our homes today.

The four homes that have been chosen for this study and the scriptures where the pertinent information can be found are the following:

The home of Simon Peter (Luke 4:38-39)

The home of Jairus (Luke 8:41-56)

The home of Mary and Martha (Luke 10:38-42)

The home of Zacchaeus (Luke 19:1-10)

Other homes and other passages could be easily considered and may, to some, be more worthy of consideration than these. I have chosen these four homes for three reasons.

First, in each home, Jesus is seen as a welcomed guest. In one of the cases mentioned above (Zacchaeus), Jesus seems to have invited Himself. Even with that, in each of the texts, Jesus appears to be welcomed by the hosts.

The second reason for looking at these four homes is that they are not all *Momonyms*. No, I did not misspell "homonyms." The word I intended to use is, in fact, *Momonyms*. A radio personality to whom I have listened in the past would often greet his callers with, "How's Momonym?"

When the question, *"How's Mom and them?"* is asked, there is basic assumption made. The assumption seems to be that there is some similarity in every home or family. At least, each family consists of *Momonym*.

This is not always the case. The family unit that lives at one particular address may be Dad, Mom, and the "traditional" two children. It may be only Mom and the kids. It may be only Dad and the children. It may be two older people living by themselves after having reared their family. It may be a young couple who have yet to have any children. It may be one person living alone. There are several possibilities.

No two families are exactly alike, even if they do have the same number of members. Families are like snowflakes; each one is unique.

The somewhat sketchy information we have been given about the four homes mentioned earlier lead us to the conclusion that they were not alike. Was there a young girl in Peter's home like there was in the home of Jairus? Did the mother of Jairus live with him and his family like what seems to have been the case in Peter's home? Did

Mary, Martha and their brother Lazarus all live in the same house? If so, were their parents living with them? When Jesus walked into the house of Zacchaeus, who was there? Was there a wife and were there children; did Lazarus live alone; were there in-laws in this house, too?

Each home (family) that welcomed Jesus was different. Each home (family) today that welcomes him is also different.

Jesus offered the homes into which He went *and* He offers homes today exactly what is needed. As the song reminds us, "My Jesus Knows Just What I Need." **This** is the third, and, in my mind, the best reason to look at these homes into which Jesus went as a guest. What He was able to bring into their homes, he can bring into our homes today.

When Jesus entered the home of Simon, He entered as *"The Great Physician."* When He came to the home of Jairus, He was coming as *"The Resurrection and the Life."* When He came to the home of Mary and Martha, He entered as *"The Master Teacher"* (with words of life). Finally, when He "invited Himself" into the home of Zacchaeus, He came as his *"Savior."* There are some important implications of this for us today.

The Great Physician Makes a House Call

First, I believe that Jesus desires to be present in our homes during times when illness is an unwelcome guest. The result of His being in our homes during these times may not be the same as the result of His being in Simon's home. That is to say that there may not be an immediate physical healing.

It is at this point that the faith of some may waver. Their reasoning may go something like this: If "Jesus Christ [is] the same yesterday, and today, and forever" (Heb. 13:8), and if He could heal Simon's mother then, why does He not immediately heal me or my loved one who is ill?

It seems appropriate at this juncture to propose the idea that, often-times, there exists a need that is far greater than the need of physical healing. For example, it may very well be that the greatest need in a particular family is the healing of a relationship.

An estranged family member may return home during a time of the severe illness of a parent or sibling. A strained relationship could be "healed." A husband may finally understand how important his wife is to him. A child may become more appreciative of the sacrifices made by his or her parent(s). A parent may realize that time spent with a child is much more important than money spent on a child. The possibilities are almost endless.

It may very well be that the relationship that is most in need of healing is one's relationship with God. The Bible affirms, and the experiences of many demonstrates, that physical difficulties can make us more appreciative of, dependent upon, and loyal to our Father.

Consider these words from the Psalmist:

Before I was afflicted I went astray, but now I keep Your word. It is good for me that I have been afflicted, that I may learn Your statutes (Psalm 119:67, 71).

The Holy Spirit inspired Paul to inform us that God may, in fact, use difficulties in our lives in order to mold us more into the image He has in mind for us:

Likewise the Spirit also helps in our weaknesses. For we do not know what we should pray for as we ought, but the Spirit Himself makes intercession for us with groanings which cannot be uttered. Now He who searches the hearts knows what the mind of the Spirit is, because He makes intercession for the saints according to the will of God. And we know that all things work together for good to those who love God, to those who are the called according to His purpose. For whom He foreknew, He also predestined to be conformed to the image of His Son, that He might be the firstborn among many brethren (Romans 8:26-29).

Paul's experience with his "thorn in the flesh" he mentions in 2 Cor. 12:7-10 is also instructive in this regard. There is no doubt about the fact that Paul believed in the power of God and that he prayed about this matter. In fact, he informs the reader that he prayed three times about this.

However, Paul did not receive immediate (or even delayed) relief. He got something far better; a greater understanding of, and appreciation for, the Lord's grace, strength, and power.

There may have been a time in your life when you can look back on some real difficulties and, from the vantage point of having made it through that valley, understand God's purpose. If you have not yet "been there," you probably will be at some point.

The Resurrection and the Life in the Home

Wouldn't it be wonderful if Jesus could come into our homes every time we lose somebody close to us and bring them back to us, just as He did for Jairus and his family? None of us expect that, but all of us need Jesus to be in our homes when death enters the home.

The Bible has many references that have comforted an untold number of people when they lose a loved one. John 14:1-4, 1 Thes. 4:13-18, and 1 Cor. 15:50-58 are but three that readily come to mind.

However, one of the most instructive may be David's response to his servants after learning of the death of the son born as a result of his sinful relationship with Bathsheba. When the servants could not understand why he was now eating and going on with his life when, before the child died, his behavior was, to say the least, erratic, his response to them was:

> ...While the child was alive, I fasted and wept; for I said, 'Who can tell whether the Lord will be gracious to me, that the child may live?' But now he is dead; why should I fast? Can I bring him back again? I shall go to him, but he shall not return to me (2 Sam. 12:22-23).

As we know, our Lord had been in the home of Mary and Martha before being there after the death of their brother, Lazarus. He was no stranger to them. In fact, it seems as though there was a special relationship between Jesus, Mary, Martha, and Lazarus.

As you may also remember, on that earlier occasion, Jesus said that Mary had "...chosen that good part, which will not be taken away from her" (Luke 10:42). That "good part" was sitting at the feet of Jesus and listening to what He had to say.

The lesson here seems to be two-fold. First, when death enters our homes, Jesus does not need to be a stranger. It helps tremendously if those who are grieving and the one who has departed have (had) a close relationship with Him.

Secondly, I am convinced that Jesus wants to be invited into our homes in order to help us to understand more of the "...the words of eternal life" (John 6:67). You may recognize that quote as coming from the lips of Peter. This, of course, follows Jesus' affirmation that "The words that I speak to you are spirit, and they are life" (John 6:63).

It is interesting to notice what Paul tells the people of Thessalonica about their departed loved ones. After some discussion that is intended to encourage them to "...sorrow as others who have no hope" (1 Thes. 4:13), the Holy Spirit inspired him to write, "Therefore comfort one another with these words" (1 Thes. 4:18). The words of Jesus and the inspired words of those who wrote the Bible can be a tremendous source of comfort during a time of loss.

I have been in two types of homes after death has made its entrance. One type has, up until that point, exhibited no interest in any spiritual matters. When death occurs, they just want a preacher to be there. Any type or "brand" will do.

The other home is the type in which Jesus is not a stranger. They are pleased to have a preacher to be with them, but there is a quiet assurance and confidence that certainly was not "brought in" by the preacher. It was already there because of a relationship with the Lord.

One of the worst things (if not **the** worst thing) anybody could do to his or her family is to leave them behind wondering about the eternal destiny of the deceased. They need to know that Jesus will welcome us into His home just as we welcomed Him into our home.

The Master Teacher Does Some "Home Schooling"

Sadly, instead of inviting Jesus and His teachings into our homes, many of us have invited His adversary and his followers right into our family rooms, living rooms and even our bedrooms. Instead of opening the Divine Book, many, instead, grab the remote or electronic device and are "entertained" with the most ungodly material imaginable.

I have long been impressed with the wording of the final verses of Hebrews 5. For quite some time, I thought that the author was trying to get the readers to make some spiritual progress and that he was saying that they had never matured.

However, I began to notice that they were criticized because "... you **have come** to need milk and not solid food" (Heb. 5:12). The implication seems to be that, at one time, they *were* making some progress, but had now regressed to spiritual infancy.

Each of us needs to resolve to be more like Mary and to take the time to get to know Jesus and His Word as well as we can. Martha needed to learn that some things can wait. Maybe I need to learn that same lesson.

Salvation in the Home

As was the case with Zacchaeus, the pressing need of every home is *salvation*. Absolutely nothing is more important than that. I wonder, as Jesus views our lives, how many times He sees one of us and says, "He/she is just like that man I talked about who had so much 'stuff' that he needed extra storage space" (cf. Luke 12:13-21)!

Of all of the "isms" that threaten God's people today, one of the most insidious ones is *materialism*. I am concerned about liberalism, anti-ism, denominationalism, legalism, etc., but far too many people are blind to their need for God because of the lure of *things*.

We read our Lord's soul-searching question over and over again, but I wonder if we ever really let it sink in. Let's read it one more time. Maybe I'll make a better application for my life and maybe I'll encourage somebody else to do the same: "For what profit is it to a man if he gains the whole world, and loses his own soul? Or what will a man give in exchange for his soul" (Matt. 16:26)?

At this point some of the "preachers" that are seen on television and heard on radios would encourage people to say some sort of "simple prayer" and ask Jesus to come into their lives. We cannot do that and remain true to His teaching.

However, we can encourage people to follow God's plan of salvation by hearing the gospel, believing that gospel, answering the challenge to repent, gladly confessing his or her faith in Jesus as the Son of God, and obeying the commandment to be baptized. We believe that the Lord will add all those who do so to the same church to which He added those who heard and obeyed the commands contained in that great sermon preached on the Day of Pentecost and during subsequent days (cf. Acts 2:47).

The church at Laodicea is remembered because it was lukewarm. It may not be as well remembered that, in the context of castigating this church, our Lord made it known that a relationship with Him is one which is personal. One of the great statements of His desire to be a guest in their homes and in my home, as well as one of the great promises to those who allow Him to be a guest, is found in Revelation 3:20-21.

We shall close this chapter with the prayer that each one who reads these words has allowed Jesus to take up residence in his or her home.

> Behold, I stand at the door and knock. If anyone hears My voice and opens the door, I will come in to him and dine with him, and he with Me. To him who overcomes I will grant to sit with Me on My throne, as I also overcame and sat down with My Father on His throne (Rev. 3:20-21).

Our Eternal Home

13

Our Eternal Home

Those of us who worship regularly can probably recall any number of songs that have to do with heaven being our home. One of the things about heaven that makes it so attractive to us is that picture; the picture of home.

One of the songs of recent years begins with these words:

> I'm kind of homesick for a country
> To which I've never been before
>
> (words & music by Squire Parsons, Jr.
> Copyright 1979; Kingsmen Publishing C. BMI)

Have you ever wondered about that? Have you ever asked yourself how anybody could be homesick for some place he/she has never been? Have you ever wondered why the idea of being home in heaven seems so appealing?

What can make a place I've never been seem like home to me?

Most of us can understand our excitement about getting to go to our earthly home after being away for an extended time. Think of the last day of a semester in college. Think of a discharge from the armed forces. Think of *anything* that meant you could finally go home after an extended time away.

It is my opinion that, if we can identify some of the things that made those experiences so special, we may begin to understand what makes the thought of our eternal home seem so special to us. At least that will be our attempt in this final chapter of this book.

I would suggest, first of all, some of the things that may not be primary among the reasons for our thinking of heaven as our home. Among these would be some of the descriptions of heaven we find in God's Word.

I believe that most of us would agree that some of what the Bible tells us could be called accommodative language. It is the Holy Spirit's way of conveying to us what must be indescribable in terms we can try to understand. For example; I'm not too sure that anybody expects to literally see something like this in heaven: "...the city was pure gold, like clear glass (Rev. 21:18). It is my belief that this description, like many of the others about heaven, are meant to convey a thought something like: "You've never seen anything like this before. You can't even begin to imagine (in the words of another song) "how beautiful heaven must be.'"

A few years ago, my wife and I went to the Biltmore House in Asheville, North Carolina. We were awed by its size, its beauty, etc. "Impressed" is not the word that would be adequate enough to describe our reaction. "Overwhelmed" would be much closer.

At the same time, nothing we saw at the Biltmore House made us feel "at home," nor do we wish it could be our home. We were very glad to get back to the place we were familiar with. Our house will never compete with the Biltmore House in ways that must have appealed to the Biltmore family, but it is "home" to us.

I would also suggest that the promise of a place where there are no tears, no sorrow, no separation, no pain, etc. sounds wonderful. At the same time, that promise doesn't make such a place feel like home. I've never been in any environment anywhere where at least some of those things did not exist.

Again, I would ask the question: How can I be homesick for some place I've never been? I would suggest three answers to that question.

First, I would suggest that **"things" make a place a home**. Aren't some of the things in your house what make it feel like home to you? How often, for example, have you been glad to finally sit in your favorite chair, sleep in your own bed, etc.? How comforting is it to see those family pictures on the wall, to know where the channels are on the television you are watching, to use your own appliances, etc.?

If you will notice, I put the word *things* in quotation marks in that last paragraph. I am not at all suggesting that we can "take it with us." Two passages in Luke are enough to substantiate that point. I am sure that most, if not all, who are reading this are familiar with the man we often call "the rich fool" (cf. Luke 12:16-21) and our Lord's account of "the rich man and Lazarus" (cf. Luke 16:19-31).

One common observation made by many is that they have never seen a hearse pulling a U-Haul trailer. According to some accounts I have read, somebody asked John D. Rockefeller's accountant, "How much did Mr. Rockefeller leave?" The answer from the accountant was, "He left all of it."

So, if material things are not the "things" I have in mind that might cause us to long for heaven as our home, what am I talking about? I have in mind the same things that our Lord had in mind when he said:

Do not lay up for yourselves treasures on the earth, where moth and rust destroy and where thieves break in and steal; but lay up for yourselves treasures in heaven, where neither moth nor rust destroys and where thieves do not break in and steal (Matt. 6:19-20).

I am also thinking of these words found in Revelation 14:13:

…'Blessed are the dead who die in the Lord from now on. 'Yes,' says the Spirit, 'that they may rest from their labors, and their works follow them (Rev. 14:13).

As one familiar song says, "This world is not my home. I'm just a-passing through. **My treasures are laid up somewhere beyond the** *blue."* In 1883, a man by the name of Charles Studd wrote a poem wherein the following words were repeated at the end of each stanza:

> Only one life, 'twill soon be past,
> Only what's done for Christ will last.

Those are the kinds of "things" that I believe will make heaven seem like home.

I would suggest that a second reason why Christians are, or at least should be, homesick for a place they have never been has to do with **the relationships that are there**.

In view of our Lord's teaching in Matthew 22:23-33 about the fact that, in heaven, we "...neither marry nor are given in marriage... (v. 30), I do not necessarily have in mind some of the relationships which are so dear to us in this present life.

It should be remembered that the apostles left their families, their means of income, and other things to follow Jesus. It is hoped that the reader will notice that the word in that last sentence is "left," not abandoned. The information that Mark provides about James and John is interesting. He records that they left their father "...with the hired servants..." (Mark 1:20). It appears that they did not leave Zebedee to fend for himself.

The fact that Peter's mother-in-law was in his house (cf. Luke 4:38) is interesting. It is yet another indication that these apostles did not turn their backs on those whom they loved.

There are, to be sure, some passages that *seem to indicate* a total abandonment and renouncing of all earthly relationships. It is my firm belief that, when studied in their context and compared with other passages of scripture, they do not, in fact, teach that.

However, what is taught very clearly is that our relationship with, and loyalty to, Jesus must eclipse any other relationship we have. It has been noted more than once that Jesus will accept nothing other than first place in our lives. If that is the relationship I have with Him now, it seems to me that the fact that I can be in His presence will be one of the reasons I want to go to heaven.

Please allow me to take this one step further. Is it not true that people committed to a common cause are also committed to one another? The men who signed their names to *The Declaration of Independence* affixed their signatures to a document that read, in part:

"We mutually pledge **to each other** our lives, our fortunes and our sacred honor" (emphasis added).

Imagine a meeting that included those people from the distant past who dreamed of, spoke of, and wrote of freedom. Imagine that this meeting also included the men who signed *The Declaration of Independence* and those who fought valiantly for our nation's freedom from England. Imagine further that this meeting would include those of us living today who are privileged to enjoy freedom. Wouldn't you long to be in a meeting like that?

What if there was a place where all who were or are committed to God could meet. This meeting would include all those who pointed to the coming of the Messiah. It would include all who were devoted to Him while He was on the earth. It would also include all who have been (and are) devoted to Him since His ascension to be with His Father. Wouldn't you long to be in a meeting like that? Wouldn't you wish it could last forever? It can and it will!

Consider these words from the lips of Jesus:

And I say to you that many will come from east and west, and sit down with Abraham, Isaac, and Jacob in the kingdom of heaven (Matt. 8:11).

It would probably be impossible to mention all of the reasons why heaven can be seen as our home. For our purposes here, I will only mention one more.

I believe that we think of heaven in terms of "home" because **that is where our Father is**. When I was a child, my longing to be at home when I was away had to do with the fact that it was where my parents were. The people who loved me, protected me, and nurtured me meant more than anything I was experiencing away from them.

It is significant that the writer of Hebrews refers to God as "... the Father of spirits..." (Heb. 12:9). It also needs to be remembered that the wise man of old informed us that, at death, "...the spirit will return to God who gave it" (Eccl. 12:7).

The writer of Hebrews also pictures Jesus as (depending on the specific text and the translation you are reading) the ---

- "author and finisher of our faith" (Heb. 12:2; (KJV & NKJV)
- "author and perfecter of our faith" (Heb. 12:2; ASV; NASVU; NIV)
- "founder and perfecter of our faith" (Heb. 12:2, ESV)

It is my understanding that the word picture used here and elsewhere in Hebrews is somewhat related to those old westerns I used to watch as a kid. In those movies and television shows, it was not unusual to send somebody ahead of the wagon train, the posse, etc. as a scout. The scout was to find the best way to get to the desired destination or person, look for potential dangers, and then come back and lead the rest of the party safely.

There can be absolutely no doubt about the fact that our Lord fills that role for us. As our older brother (cf. Heb. 2:11), He has both the relationship with us and the experience to lead. He has shown us the way. In fact He *is* the way (cf. John 14:6). He is already where we desire to go. He is at home with His Father. He desires for us to join him there.

Please allow me to close this material that has discussed some matters dealing with homes, families, and relationships with my prayer for those who have read the material. It is my prayer that each one who reads any of this will find something to help him or her to have a wonderful, Christian family. It is my prayer that each one will enjoy a rich relationship with his or her spouse, parents, children and any others in the family.

However, even more than that I pray that each one of us will become and/or be Christians in the New Testament sense of that word. I can think of no better way to end this book than with the inspired words below from Paul:

...I bow my knees to the Father of our Lord Jesus Christ, from whom the whole family in heaven and earth is named, that He would grant you, according to the riches of His glory, to be strengthened with might through His Spirit in the inner man, that Christ may dwell in your hearts through faith; that you, being rooted and grounded in love, may be able to comprehend with all the saints what is the width and length and depth and height — to know the love of Christ which passes knowledge; that you may be filled with all the fullness of God.

Now to Him who is able to do exceedingly abundantly above all that we ask or think, according to the power that works in us, to Him be glory in the church by Christ Jesus to all generations, forever and ever. Amen (Eph. 3:14-20).

Made in the USA
San Bernardino, CA
01 September 2016